Advance Praise for Me

I am one of those friends, colleagues, and social media connections who followed Chris's devotional thoughts on Mark. Actually, I began to eagerly anticipate them. They struck a nerve for me with their simplicity, freshness, and transparency. Chris is a gifted writer, and I am so thankful that he has finally published *Meditations on Mark*.

—Joel Thrasher
Missions Strategy Leader

As a superb story teller himself, Chris, in his *Meditations on Mark*, has captured the essence of Mark's stories about Jesus. Reading these devotionals one can almost hear the still, small voice of God's Spirit. Readers are challenged and inspired to allow the life of Jesus to shape their own lives.

If I were to use one-word comments about *Meditations on Mark*, they would be words like *insightful* and *inspirational, touching* and *timely*.

—Dr. Jack Causey
Ministerial Transitions Coordinator
Cooperative Baptist Fellowship of North Carolina

Smyth & Helwys Publishing, Inc.
6316 Peake Road
Macon, Georgia 31210-3960
1-800-747-3016
©2016 by Chris Cadenhead

Library of Congress Cataloging-in-Publication Data

Names: Cadenhead, Chris.
Title: Meditations on Mark : daily devotions from the oldest Gospel / by
Chris Cadenhead.
Description: Macon, Georgia : Smyth & Helwys Publishing, Inc., 2016.
Identifiers: LCCN 2015045719 | ISBN 9781573128513 (pbk. : alk. paper)
Subjects: LCSH: Bible. Mark--Meditations. | Bible. Mark--Devotional use.
Classification: LCC BS2585.54 .C34 2016 | DDC 242/.5--dc23
LC record available at http://lccn.loc.gov/2015045719

Meditations
on Mark

DAILY DEVOTIONS *from* **THE OLDEST GOSPEL**

CHRIS CADENHEAD

*To Mom and Dad,
who from an early age showed me
a life shaped by Scripture.*

*To Heather,
who has always blessed and encouraged
the way our family is shaped by ministry.*

Acknowledgments

I once heard it said that a person who thinks he is leading when no one is following is just taking a walk. It's as true of the pastorate as it is of any other vocation. Vocational ministry requires both an internal and an external call. Internally, someone has to sense God's call on his or her life. Externally, the church has to confirm that call by affirming the gifts and abilities it perceives in the individual. On the evening of February 22, 1998, the people of the First Baptist Church of High Point, North Carolina, came forward and laid their hands on me to place their blessings on my bizarre claim that God wanted me to come work for Him in His church. As amazed as I have been since then that God called me to vocational ministry, I have been equally amazed that there have been congregations willing to vouch for that call by allowing me the privilege of being their pastor!

I am grateful to the congregations that have been home to my family during these last eighteen years of ministry. The First Baptist Church of Mt. Gilead, North Carolina; Augusta Road Baptist Church in Greenville, South Carolina; and Bayshore Baptist Church in Tampa, Florida, all took a chance and called me to be their pastor. Each congregation taught me something important about myself and my calling. Just as importantly, each congregation has blessed me with friendships that continue to enrich my life. Most recently, Bonsack Baptist Church in Roanoke, Virginia, has given me the chance to participate in an unprecedented approach to pastoral succession as Dr. Bob Moore prepares to retire from forty years of leading this church on a path of continuous growth. He has been the kind of friend and mentor that every pastor needs.

One thing that has been clear to me in every congregation I have served has been the centrality of Scripture. In every church I have called home the Bible has been preached, taught, discussed, debated, argued, prayed, sung, and adored. Any time I have been tempted to allow my ministry to drift off into the realms of social commentary or political opinion, I have been greeted on Sunday morning by faces of my church peering back at me, anxious to hear some word from the Lord. These brothers and sisters in Christ have lovingly reminded me that regardless of how interesting I happen to think my opinions are, they want to know what God has to say.

This book of devotional readings, then, is born out of my experience with the people of the church of Jesus Christ. I am grateful for the way they have encouraged—perhaps even required—me to stay grounded in the revealed truth of Scripture. The church keeps driving me back to the realization that, apart from the word of God, I have nothing of value to offer it. Without the Bible, the preacher is just another talking head. With the Bible the church is never boring! It is my prayer that this collection of readings enriches the church's love of Scripture.

Contents

Introduction   ix

Mark 1:1-8   1

Mark 1:9-13   3

Mark 1:14-20   5

Mark 1:21-28   7

Mark 1:29-34   9

Mark 1:35-39   11

Mark 1:40-45   13

Mark 2:1-12   15

Mark 2:13-17   17

Mark 2:18-22   19

Mark 2:23–3:6   21

Mark 3:7-12   23

Mark 3:13-19   25

Mark 3:20-30   27

Mark 3:31-35   29

Mark 4:1-20   31

Mark 4:21-25   33

Mark 4:26-29   35

Mark 4:30-34   37

Mark 4:35-41   39

Mark 5:1-20   41

Mark 5:21-43   43

Mark 6:1-6a   45

Mark 6:6b-13   47

Mark 6:14-29   49

Mark 6:30-44   51

Mark 6:45-56   53

Mark 7:1-23   55

Mark 7:24-30   57

Mark 7:31-37   59

Mark 8:1-13   61

Mark 8:14-21   63

Mark 8:22-26   65

Mark 8:27-30   67

Mark 8:31–9:1   69

Mark 9:2-13   71
Mark 9:14-32   73
Mark 9:33-37   75
Mark 9:38-41   77
Mark 9:42-50   79
Mark 10:1-12   81
Mark 10:13-16   83
Mark 10:17-31   85
Mark 10:32-34   87
Mark 10:35-45   89
Mark 10:46-52   91
Mark 11:1-11   93
Mark 11:12-19   95
Mark 11:20-26   97
Mark 11:27-33   99
Mark 12:35-40   101
Mark 12:41-44   103
Mark 13:1-2   105
Mark 13:3-31   107
Mark 14:1-11   109
Mark 14:12-26   111
Mark 14:27-31   113
Mark 14:32-42   115
Mark 14:43-52   117
Mark 14:53-65   119
Mark 14:66-72   121
Mark 15:1-15   123
Mark 15:16-20   125
Mark 15:21-32   127
Mark 15:33-38   129
Mark 15:42-47   131
Mark 16:1-8   133
Mark 16:9-20   135

Introduction

Sometimes the most interesting experiences in life are the ones you did not set out to find. This book falls into that category. What you are reading began as a personal undertaking that I had no intention of publishing. I was merely seeking to bring a little discipline and order to my devotional life, and yet along the way friends began suggesting that I make my thoughts and reflections available to others. On a whim I mailed off a sampling, and now you are holding a copy in your hands!

It began in early spring 2014. My family and I had just made the difficult but exciting decision to accept a call to a new place of ministry in another state. It was difficult because it meant saying good-bye to friends we had come to cherish, but it was exciting because it presented me with an opportunity to pursue some unspoken personal and professional needs. It is amazing how God sometimes grants the desires of our hearts before we even name them to ourselves, much less to others.

Anticipating how chaotic life would get in the coming weeks as the time for the move drew closer, I decided to commit to something that I felt would help keep me spiritually grounded. A friend and colleague had recently convinced me to start making more use of social media for ministry purposes, so I tweeted (on the social media application known as Twitter) that I would regularly post online devotionals for anyone who cared to read them. At the time I didn't have many social media "friends" or "followers," so I had no grand illusions that my postings would be widely read, but I felt like making that announcement would hold me accountable to follow through with my promise. If I were ever tempted to overlook my daily devotional time, I simply remembered that a handful of others had read their pastor's commitment that he was going to do it!

Of course, accountability wasn't my only motivation. Social media notwithstanding, I find great value in the discipline of writing. Writing helps me to clarify and focus my thoughts. The weekly experience of sermon writing, for example, is for me just that—an exercise in clarification. Plenty of preachers do well working from a series of bullet points or topical outlines and then adding the meat to the bones as they stand in the pulpit to proclaim God's word, but I am not one of them. I work best through writing out my manuscript almost word for word, paying careful attention to sentence structure and the flow from one paragraph to the next. I will leave it to those who must endure listening to me every week to decide whether that makes me a better preacher, but it is without a doubt my comfort zone.

I figured my personal devotional life could benefit from the same discipline. Rather than simply thinking about a particular text of Scripture, I decided to put my thoughts into words. Doing so would require me to focus on some aspect of the passage rather than allowing it to mean anything and everything all at the same time. It would also allow me to go back at any point and read what I had written to get a sense of where I was on my journey with Christ at a particular moment. Knowing that a potential handful of others might read my thoughts once I posted them motivated me to make sure that what I wrote was minimally coherent.

I decided to base the writings on a continual reading through the Gospel of Mark. Many devotional guides effectively move in an unsystematic way from one topic or theme or Scripture to the next. Each reflection expresses what was going on in the author's heart or the mind at the time. But I wanted to be more systematic. Not convinced that I would spontaneously have some thought worth sharing each day, I wanted to move passage by passage through a book of the Bible, letting the Scriptures instead of my own personal musings form the basis of my reflections.

I chose Mark for three reasons. First, it is the shortest of the Gospels, making it possible that I might get all the way through the book in a reasonable time. Second, Mark has a sense of urgency. He moves quickly through the story of Jesus' life, relying on a series of brief passages that often begin with the phrase "and then . . . ." It is as though Mark has some important ending to which he is in a hurry to arrive (which, of course, he does). The terseness of Mark's style seemed to lend itself to the kinds of brief reflections I hoped to offer. Finally, scholarly consensus is that Mark is the oldest of the four Gospels. I found it spiritually engaging to reflect daily on the first known effort to summarize and proclaim the life and ministry of Jesus.

That's where this began, and at first that's all it was. I didn't know for sure whether the handful of people connected to me through social media were paying attention, but eventually my posts started to gain momentum. As the date of our move got closer, people in my new congregation wanted to know more about this guy who was coming to be their pastor, and my postings seemed to be a good way for them to indulge their curiosity. Every day I received new friend requests. Whereas I started with a few dozen, I now have close to 500. I realize this hardly qualifies me for the social media hall of fame, but it did suggest that I was on to something. When several people suggested I consider publishing these devotions, it further confirmed my suspicion that I had struck a nerve.

That nerve is connected, I think, to a desire for a fresh encounter with Scripture. I have no delusions that what I offer in these devotions represents any kind of earth-shattering originality. There is nothing here that countless others before me have not already thought or written. Authentic spirituality does not mean coming up with something nobody has ever thought before. To the contrary, we can only truly experience God when we read Scripture in concert with the entire community of faith, and that includes those who have gone before us. I once heard it said that true creativity means forgetting where you heard it the first time. (I can't remember who said that!) I hope that the saints of the past would be pleased with what I have written.

While we don't need to be overly innovative, we do need to think beyond the platitudes, clichés, and truisms that we so readily associate with Scripture. When every reading of the Bible ends with a nice saying that smells like potpourri and fits easily on a bumper sticker, then you can be sure that we have lost the richness, the layered nuances, and the penetrating sharpness of God's word. If anything

I have written here helps someone rediscover even a razor's width of that edginess, then I will consider the project a success.

I hope what I offer is at least consistent with what our best and most faithful scholars say to us. While this book is not intended to offer biblical commentary, if preachers and teachers find anything here that is useful or inspirational in the work they do, then I will be well pleased. This is merely intended to be a helpful and friendly guide to personal mediation and prayer.

To that end, the reader should feel free to use this book in any way that is beneficial. If that means reading it straight through or even using it as a shim to straighten your Christmas tree, then more power to you. (I have a couple of small paperbacks on the shelves in our den that exist purely for that purpose.) But I suggest that the book will be most helpful if used in the way it was created—as a series of daily devotional readings.

Each entry begins with a Scripture reference that merely picks up where the previous reading concluded. The reader is encouraged first to read the passage from the Bible, noticing and reflecting on whatever themes or images seem to catch the attention. Read with a spirit of trust that God really does have something to say us. Then the reader can find my personal reflection on that passage to see if it aids his or her own reflection. Finally, there is a concluding prayer. I cannot say it enough: the written reflections and the prayers are intended to be a stimulant and not a substitute for the reader's personal meditations.

The Christian life is both communal and private. It is communal in that Christ has called us together. We follow him in community with one another, so we must avoid the temptation to see the spiritual life as purely a private matter between "me and Jesus." No devotional guide should ever be used as a replacement for regular, disciplined participation in the life of the church. At the same time, the community can only be as strong and mature as each of us are willing to commit ourselves to being. We must each do the disciplined work of listening and responding to God's voice that comes to us through the word—the Bible. My prayer is that what you find on these pages will be useful to that end.

Mark 1:1-8

"He will baptize you with the Holy Spirit."

This is the promise John the Baptist makes in the opening chapter of Mark's Gospel. Mark doesn't begin with the story of Jesus' birth. Rather, he jumps into the middle of the story with Jesus already as an adult, ready to begin his ministry. This is the urgency in Mark: The Messiah has come. Everything is about to change. Get ready. So the first words in Mark are not from an angel announcing a mysterious birth; they are from a fiery prophet named John who is calling people to repentance. It's time to make a change. God is about to show up in an unprecedented way, so get ready. Repent.

We must be careful not to confuse repentance with a simple act of human will, as in "I'm going to try harder to do better." The fact is, we can't. Sin is too much of a reality in our lives. Our efforts at self-improvement will meet with limited success at best. Tell yourself that this time you are definitely going to get into shape. And then remind yourself of that promise a week later when you are sitting on the sofa eating a cheeseburger. Or, more important, tell yourself that you are not going to think any negative or critical thoughts about other people, and then check back in a few hours to see how you did. "So I find this law at work: Although I want to do good, evil is right there with me," says the Apostle Paul in Romans 7:21.

That's why this promise from John the Baptist is so important. True repentance requires the work of the Holy Spirit. Apart from the living God coming to live inside of us, we will never make the changes we need to make. Repentance, then, is more than a form of behavior modification, as important as that may be. It is an act of inviting the Holy Spirit to enter into our lives. It is acknowledging that we need God to do for us what we cannot do for ourselves. It is not enough simply to attempt to get rid of the bad stuff, because other bad stuff will take its place. We must also become a dwelling place for the Holy Spirit.

Prepare the way for the Lord.

Holy God, I acknowledge my frustrations and failures at becoming the person I want to be. The temptation to sin is too great, too pervasive. Come into my life today. Shine your holy light on the darkness that resides inside of me, and create a space for your dwelling. Make me into someone who is prepared for the arrival of God. Through Christ, Amen.

Mark 1:9-13

As I write these words the church is in the forty-day season of Lent, which draws its symbolic structure from the forty days Jesus spent in the wilderness. Mark's account of this event is brief and lacking in detail compared to the accounts given by Matthew and Luke, but he still has this story at the beginning of his Gospel. In fact, we haven't yet heard Jesus say a word, but here we have him being driven by the Holy Spirit into the wilderness to face temptation. (Literally translated, the original Greek says that the Holy Spirit threw him out into the wilderness.) This is Mark saying, "You can't get to the good news of the gospel until you go through the desert."

That's because the desert is a bare place. In the desert, all the distractions and creature comforts are stripped away, and you are forced to confront yourself and come to terms with who you really are. This was at the heart of Jesus' temptation. He had come into the world to do the Father's work. But how exactly would he complete that mission? Satan was offering him alternative ways to define his purpose. Power, security, wealth—these things could be Jesus' if only he would yield to what Satan was asking. These things are a long way from the path of service, suffering, and sacrifice that the Father had laid out before him. They were temptations indeed.

But Jesus rejected them. He chose to stay true to his vocation as the obedient and suffering servant. He would not let the ways of the world define either his mission or how he accomplished it.

We face the same temptations all the time. Temptation is more than just the occasional (or frequent) impulse to break a rule or do a wrong thing. It's deeper than that. Temptation is the tendency to define our lives on terms other than God's. We too have been called to a life of service and sacrifice and, yes, suffering love. And when our lives are said and done, we will be measured not by how many accomplishments we have achieved or how high up the ladder we have climbed or how beautiful we kept our home or how much other people liked us. We will be measured by how faithful we have been to our vocation as the children of God—children who have been called to follow our Lord on his path to the cross.

Holy God, thank you that when Jesus faced the temptations of Satan, he stood firm and steadfast. Just as much, thank you that on the cross he substituted your faithfulness for my waywardness. Give me insight this day to recognize the temptations that come my way. And by your strength, help me to stand firm in your love. Through Christ, Amen.

Mark 1:14-20

I grew up in a Christian home, so my coming to faith was a gradual process. Over time I grew into the faith to which I was exposed from my earliest days. For others the conversion experience is more sudden and dramatic—something more in line with what happens to the Apostle Paul in Acts 9.

No matter the timeline or the process of conversion, for all believers there is immediacy to the call of Christ. Even for me there came a moment when the truth of the gospel broke into my young life, and I realized there was something I was supposed to do with it. Better said, there came a moment when I realized that the message I had been hearing all my life wanted to do something with me. In that moment Jesus became more than an idea or even a person; he became the Truth who was asking me for a response.

The call of the first disciples was immediate. In some ways, Peter and Andrew and James and John had spent their entire lives preparing for this moment. As faithful Jews, they had been taught from their earliest days that God would send the chosen one to come and set the people free. Yet nothing could have fully prepared them for this moment, for Jesus didn't exactly match up with anyone's expectations. He intercepted them on their normal path and sent their lives careening off in a new direction they could have never predicted.

The way Mark tells it, Jesus simply walks up and says, "Follow me." There is no effort to connect that call to some deep longing or some previous experience. Jesus doesn't say, "Dear friend, I understand that you have been searching for deeper meaning in life. Why don't you come with me and see if that does the trick?" He doesn't say, "I hear you've been questioning whether God is real. Come and let me show you." The call of Christ is not stated as a response to some need on Peter's part. The call is simply made. "Follow me."

The call of Christ comes with its own inner authority. Jesus has no need to make that call fit into our preconceived ideas. He is not obligated to present himself as the answer to whatever questions we have decided to ask. He simply calls us. Just as the resurrection could not have been predicted on the basis of anyone's previous experience, the very call of the gospel interrupts and disrupts our settled lives. Jesus still says, "Follow me."

Everything hinges on what we do with that invitation.

Lord Jesus, forgive me for all the ways that I try to squeeze you into my neat little boxes. Set me free this day to hear again your liberating call to come and follow you. Enable me to hear your call on your terms, instead of insisting that it come on mine. Thank you that you continue to call us today. By the power of your resurrection, Amen.

Mark 1:21-28

My seminary professors taught me a lot of important things, but how to perform a demon exorcism was not one of them. When I was actually called on to do one, I found myself way out of my comfort zone!

In January 2013, I was in India with a team of other pastors and teachers for the purpose of conducting a two-week training seminar for local Indian pastors. While we visited in one of their churches, a woman began lurching and shaking and making guttural sounds. When the pastor of the church asked me through an interpreter to lay hands on her and pray the demon out, I was quite intimidated. Sheepishly I touched her head and began praying, though I can't remember exactly *what* I prayed. At that point I was relying on the Apostle Paul's promise in Roman 8:26—"In the same way, the Spirit helps us in our weakness. We do not know what we ought to pray for, but the Spirit himself intercedes for us with groans that words cannot express." Others from the church gathered around and added their prayers to mine. The sound of our languages mixing together in that small church was a true Pentecost-like experience (read Acts 2). A few moments later the woman was calm and appeared to be in her right mind. She sat up and the service continued.

The New Testament does not attribute every ailment to demons. Ancient people *did* have a concept of good old-fashioned bodily sickness. But they also had a concept of the reality of spiritual evil, a fact manifested in the various confrontations Jesus has with demons in the Gospel accounts. We in the Western world have worked hard to separate the material from the spiritual, so we don't know what to do with these stories. But the Bible does not recognize that distinction. The Bible simply recognizes that there is creation, and that all of creation—both the material and the spiritual—is subject to sin and evil. And Jesus is victorious over it all.

My Indian friends seemed quite comfortable with this. They didn't seem especially disturbed when a woman fell out with demon possession during an otherwise normal worship gathering. They weren't nonchalant; they took her seriously and prayed over her with fervor. But they also treated her experience as something to which they were thoroughly prepared to respond in faith.

Demons may not present themselves in our world the same way they do in that world. The problem with evil is that it often knows how to disguise itself. But evil is evil. This morning as I drove into the office, I listened to the story of a former prostitute who is working to help young women in her town who are trapped by the sex trade.

Ask her if demons are real.

Lord Jesus, you conquered demons, healed diseases, quieted storms, and raised the dead. Help me to recognize the evil that is at work in my life today. And by your power, help me to cast it out. Amen.

Mark 1:29-34

Jesus heals Simon Peter's mother-in-law—his first miraculous healing—and suddenly he is inundated with people coming to him for a miracle of their own. It is a testimony to our brokenness and neediness. We who would like to believe we are self-sufficient are called to see ourselves in this story. If we were truly honest about ourselves, and if we were truly willing to recognize the power Jesus demonstrates in this story, we too would be flocking to him with our needs. As the old hymn puts, "Oh what peace we often forfeit, Oh what needless pain we bear, all because will not carry everything to God in prayer."

But this story ends with an interesting twist: Jesus forbids the demons he exorcizes from speaking about him. This is the first episode in what will be a pattern for Jesus in Mark's Gospel. Scholars call it the "messianic secret"—the idea that Jesus wants to delay the full revealing of his true identity.

With the advantage of hindsight that we enjoy as modern readers of the text, we can see that this pattern is connected to the cross. Jesus' true identity and the true nature of his mission cannot be understood until after the crucifixion. Yes, Jesus has power over all things, including sickness and demons, but his purpose was to be more than a divine genie in a bottle who came to fix whatever was hurting at the moment. He came to take all the sin and brokenness of the world and bear it on the cross. The miracles Jesus performs along the way are important; they tell us something important about who he is. But his work will not truly be complete until he suffers and dies for the sins of the world. Only then will true healing be possible.

Sometimes God answers our prayers in the way we hope. Sometimes diseases are healed and crises are solved. Other times they are not. But the gospel calls us to see all these events in light of the ultimate triumph that Jesus wins on the cross. Whatever your needs are today, in this moment, you can rest assured that God has power over them. Just as important, you can rest assured that the risen Christ has already triumphed over them.

Lord Jesus, help me today to be honest about my needs. Save me from the foolish pride of believing that I have the power or the wisdom to fix my own life, for without you I am truly helpless. At the same time, help me today to see my present needs in light of your eternal victory. By your power I pray, Amen.

Mark 1:35-39

I confess that prayer is hard for me. Other aspects of the spiritual life come more easily. For example, I can spend hours poring over a passage of Scripture to prepare for a sermon and feel stimulated by it. Likewise, I am fulfilled in ministry by visiting the sick in the hospital, by planning a worship service, or even by returning emails in response to an action plan coming from a recent committee meeting. The active parts of the spiritual life fit my task-oriented personality.

But the minute I try to sit down in prayer, my mind immediately starts to wonder off towards all the other things I need to do. And between my family, my church family, and all the "stuff" I own, there is never a shortage of other things I need to do. Isn't the kingdom better off if I get on with the tasks before me? Let the contemplatives take care of the prayer life.

Unfortunately, Jesus won't let me off the hook that easy. My compulsion to always be *doing* is evidence of the extent to which I still have not surrendered full control of my life to God. The heart of the spiritual life is growing into our awareness of our complete and utter dependence on the Lord. Even Jesus, who had more to do than anyone ever has, found it necessary to draw away and simply be with his Father. Likewise, I have to learn to trust that the universe is not going to come to a screeching halt if I draw away for a little while and "do nothing" but pray.

James Finley writes about a lesson he once learned from Thomas Merton, a Trappist monk and spiritual writer:

> Merton told me once to quit trying so hard in prayer. He said: How does an apple ripen? It just sits in the sun. A small green apple cannot ripen in one night by tightening all its muscles, squinting its eyes and tightening its jaw in order to find itself the

next morning miraculously large, red, ripe, and juicy beside its small green counterparts. Like the birth of a baby or the opening of a rose, the birth of the true self takes place in God's time. We must wait for God, we must be awake, we must trust in God's hidden action within us.[1]

Lord Jesus, forgive me for all the ways I continue to withhold full surrender to you. Forgive me of my arrogance in assuming that it is all up to me to make things work out right. Give me the patience to trust in your goodness, which your Father will reveal in good time. Teach me to pray. And teach me to wait on your answers. By your power I pray, Amen.

Note

1. As quoted in *A Guide to Prayer for Ministers and Other Servants*, ed. Rueben P. Job and Norman Shawchuck (Nashville: The Upper Room, 1983) 77.

Mark 1:40-45

During the months of my engagement to my wife, a woman in the church I was serving at the time gave me a bit of advice. "Remember to always touch each other," she said. Then she quickly added, "I don't necessarily mean in a sexual way. I am just talking about a simple touch, just to let each other know you're there." She went on to talk about how she and her late husband had been "touchers," and how it had helped them maintain a spirit of tenderness and openness towards each other.

There is power in a simple touch—and not just between married spouses. I think this is one reason that hugs are a common way of greeting each other at church. Something within us longs for connection with other human beings, and the sensation of flesh touching flesh helps to reinforce that connection.

Unfortunately, many factors work to sever that connection. Because of sin, the world is in the business of pushing us away from each other. As one of my seminary professors used to put it, the world would love nothing better than to make us all strangers. That way we can more easily use each other for selfish purposes.

That's why I am intrigued by a simple detail in today's reading. Jesus healed a leper by reaching out and touching him. Leprosy made people untouchable in the ancient world. Lepers were considered to be cut off from the rest of society. They were isolated socially and spiritually. But Jesus refused to honor the distinctions and the divisions that defined his world—and ours. He reached out and touched a man with leprosy. And by the power of that simple touch from the Son of God, the man was healed.

Leprosy is still around in parts of the world. The ministries of Serve Trust in Narasaraopet, India, for example, have created a home for lepers. I have been there in person and have seen with my own eyes the power of a simple human connection. These are people who were previously living under a tree because no one in their society would have anything to do with them.

Even in areas where leprosy is eradicated there are people we have designated as "untouchable." Social, economic, class, gender, health, and a host of other distinctions have divided our world and made us strangers to each other. Ask yourself today: Is there anyone whom Jesus would not touch?

Lord Jesus, thank you that you did not honor the distinctions of our sinful world. Help me to see all people as created in your image. Thank you for those who have touched me. Help me now to pass along that same blessing to others. Amen.

Mark 2:1-12

"Which is easier: to say to the paralytic, 'Your sins are forgiven,' or to say, 'Get up, take your mat and walk'?"

When I was younger, this question posed a problem for me. That's because in my young adult years I went through a period of significant doubt. I never gave up my faith. I was in church every Sunday and Wednesday. I even sang in the church choir! But for a time I was assaulted by the constant threat of disbelief.

The miracle stories didn't exactly help my struggle. A graduate student in the social sciences at the time, I struggled to prove that I was rational, intelligent, and firmly in touch with reality. What was I supposed to do with "fantastical" stories of miraculous healings? Could a scientifically minded person really believe such things? The answer to Jesus' question was obvious to me in those days: of course it was harder to say "Get up and walk." Such things just don't happen!

Twenty years later I am at a different place on my journey. I still want to be considered rational and intelligent. I still revere science and believe we ought to apply our best critical-thinking skills to our investigation of the universe. A believer should have nothing to fear from honest, empirical inquiry. But the stories of the miracles no longer pose a challenge to my thought world. I can't "prove" them any more now than I could then, but I no longer feel an obligation to do so. I have come to realize that the purpose of Scripture is to narrate a different view of the world than the one that is immediately available to our senses. If the Bible unfolded only according to the "rules" that define our everyday life, then it wouldn't be worth reading. The Bible offers hope to us precisely because it dares to suggest that there is a power at work among us that transcends the limits of what we have already decided is possible. If clinging to that hope makes me appear irrational to some, then so be it.

So the answer to Jesus' question has changed for me. Sick people get up and walk all the time. To paraphrase one of my seminary professors, God heals people every day, but we spend millions of dollars a year teaching them to attribute it to a well-run health care system.

Miracles are still a big deal when they happen, but the biggest miracle of all is the miracle of forgiveness. There is a lot of suffering in the world, much of it physical. The Scriptures reveal a God who can and sometimes does intervene to alleviate these physical struggles. But much of the suffering we face comes from a deeper source. As fallen creatures, we live in a state of enmity. We are at odds with everyone and everything—with our friends, our families, our neighbors, our environment, and even with ourselves. And much of the physical suffering we face is a result of this enmity. How much sickness and pain could be alleviated if we all truly loved our neighbors as ourselves!

By the power of his word, Jesus sometimes says, "Get up and walk." But by the power of his cross, Jesus has already said, "Your sins are forgiven." We are already set free. We already have the greatest healing we could ever need.

Lord Jesus, teach me today to see that my greatest need is for forgiveness. Teach me to truly weep over my sins and to cry out to you for mercy. Thank you that you have already offered to heal me of my greatest wound. By the power of your name, Amen.

Mark 2:13-17

I remember reading that one of the best pieces of evidence for the truth of the gospel is that it is such an unlikely story. If someone were going to invent a story, they would most likely invent something different than what we have in Scripture. We would create something more in line with our assumptions and expectations, which the gospel completely ignores.

Take the disciples, for example. If we were to create a story about a god coming to earth with the purpose of rounding up a group of people to go out with him and conquer the world, what kind of people would we have him choose? People of brilliance or strength or high accomplishment—these would be the logical characteristics. But Jesus calls ordinary people, a strange choice given the extraordinary task they will undertake.

In fact, we may say they were even less than ordinary. Levi was a tax collector. The thought of taxes may not evoke warm feelings for us when April 15 rolls around each year, but in the days of Jesus, tax collectors were more than an unpopular group of people; they were known crooks. Tax collectors were Jews who willingly worked in cahoots with the Roman government to fleece their own people. Tax collectors were despised by their countrymen, and for good reason.

And Jesus calls one of them to be a disciple? Exactly what kind of movement is he starting?

It will take the rest of the gospel story to answer that question. For now, the takeaway seems pretty simple: if Levi can be a disciple, anybody can be a disciple. Even me. I'm not a known crook, but I have more faults and foibles than I care to admit. And yet Jesus still sees fit to call someone like me.

Our calling as disciples has much less to do with us than it does with God. We are not called because of our merit but because of God's. As the Apostle Paul later writes in 2 Corinthians 4:7, "We have this treasure in jars of clay to show that this all-surpassing power is from God and not from us." A clay jar is a fragile thing, but by the grace of God our fragility becomes a place for God's power to reveal itself to the world.

The good news is that if Levi can be a disciple, so can we. The bad news is that if Levi can be a disciple, we no longer have any excuses!

Lord Jesus, thank you that you have seen fit to call someone like me to follow you. Forgive me of all the excuses I make for why I cannot do what you have asked. Help me to trust that your power working through me is greater than my weakness and faults. By your power I pray, Amen.

Mark 2:18-22

Scripture often functions at multiple levels of truth. That is certainly true with today's reading. Taken as a whole, the deeper meaning of the passage concerns the relationship between the old and the new. Jesus is the bearer of the new covenant. The new covenant reinterprets and reapplies the old covenant on new terms that now include the Gentiles. And yet it does not completely abolish the old covenant. As Jesus says in Matthew 5:17, he came not to overturn the law but to fulfill it. Jesus is doing a new thing, but the new thing completes the old thing, a fact that is always important given the constantly changing circumstances of our lives.

On the surface, however, another equally important truth plays out in this passage. Jesus is criticized for not insisting that his disciples fast like the Pharisees and the disciples of John do. He responds by saying that now is the not the time to fast, for in him the kingdom of God has become present. There will, however, be a time of fasting to come when he, the bridegroom, is taken away—words that foreshadow his sacrificial death on the cross.

Life is a mixture of times of mourning and times of celebration. We would love to have lots of the latter and none of the former, but it doesn't work that way. Tragedy, hardship, crises, difficulty, sadness— these things are going to come. They are the consequences of living in a world marred by sin and brokenness. We need look no further than the cross to be reminded of this. The crucifixion stands as a constant reminder of the tragic side of life.

That's why we need a faith that equips us for navigating such times. We do not come to Jesus because we hope that he will provide some magic power that shields us from hard things. We come to Jesus because he faced those hard things head-on and bore them in his flesh to a cross. And then he came out alive on the other side!

We need not be ashamed of the joys that come our way. We should celebrate goodness and claim it as a gift. But we should also recognize that the majority of the biblical psalms are expressions of lament or grief or anguish. Authentic faith gives us a place to put our grief because we know that through Christ, God will have the last word, and it will be good.

Almighty God, give me the courage to be honest about the things that weigh me down, and save me from the foolish tendency of always trying to convince the world that everything is fine and I have it all under control. But also help me not to grieve as those who have no hope. Rather, invade even my sadness with the promise of new life in you. Through Christ, Amen.

Mark 2:23–3:6

It might be tempting to characterize Jesus as a rebel and a renegade. Perhaps one reason he has been popular among people who dislike structures and institutions is that he sometimes comes across as anti-authoritarian, someone who thumbs his nose at stuffy old religious leaders with their stuffy old rules.

But this is a misrepresentation of the gospel story. Take today's reading. Jesus gets in trouble with the Pharisees for what appears to be a violation of the Sabbath rules. In short, he "works" on the Sabbath, first by plucking grain to feed hungry disciples and then by healing a man with a disability. And those who resent having "rules" imposed on them immediately applaud.

But a closer reading will show that Jesus does not violate the fourth commandment at all. Far to the contrary, he fulfills it. The Sabbath commandment was about freedom from oppression, whether the oppression of work (Exod 20:8-11), the oppression of human injustice (Deut 5:15), or—according to the actions of Jesus—any other form of oppression. What we have in today's reading is not a case of Jesus flexing his muscle and using his divine authority to trump a rule. What we have is Jesus embodying the highest purpose for which that rule was given in the first place. The commandments were not given to restrict human freedom; they were given to safeguard that freedom and to ensure that humanity will flourish at the highest level. Jesus doesn't bend the rule to fit the situation; he takes the commandment beyond the mere written code and "enfleshes" or incarnates its true intent.

When you compare his action to ours, our selfishness is immediately obvious. We routinely play loose with the moral structures of life, but we rarely do so for the purpose of incarnating their true purposes. Usually, we do it for the sake of favoring our needs and wants in the moment, whether it's bending the truth in our conversation with others, allowing our minds to harbor resentful or lustful thoughts, misrepresenting ourselves on our income tax returns, or any of a thousand other ways that we bend the rules in our direction. We creatively justify such actions. After all, didn't Jesus set us free from the law?

Not exactly. Jesus set us free from the dead and lifeless way of legalism. But we aren't just set free *from* something; we are set free *for* something. We are set free to pursue the heart of God and the good of our neighbor.

For Jesus, this meant giving up his life on a cross.

Holy God, help me to see all the ways that I deceive myself about my own goodness. Reveal the places where I am not honoring your commandments. Help me to pursue the highest purpose for which your law was given. And thank you that you have set me free. Through Christ I pray, Amen.

Mark 3:7-12

Jesus' ministry is beginning to gain momentum. Apparently word is spreading, and people are increasingly excited about what they hear. The crowd is swelling as more and more people gather around Jesus, most of them hoping to receive a miracle of their own. This would seem to be the very image of success. The movement is growing.

Yet Jesus remains surprisingly ambivalent about it all. He doesn't dismiss or reject the crowd. He receives them without complaint and goes busily about the work of ministering to their needs. But at the same time, he doesn't celebrate his growing mass appeal. He doesn't thump his chest or point to the heavens with a sign of victory as if to say, "Yes, Father, we've done it. This is what I came here to do!"

Because it wasn't. The irony in this passage is that despite Jesus' growing popularity, only the demons truly recognize who he is. While Jesus doesn't disparage the crowds or blame them for seeking relief from their suffering, he also knows that he did not come into the world just to meet people's immediate needs. He didn't come to gather a crowd of fans. He came to make the ultimate sacrifice and to build a community of disciples who are committed to sharing in that sacrifice. Jesus' ministry is defined by the cross, not by the crowds.

What is our definition of success? Whether in business or in family life or even in ministry, it is tempting to base our assessments of ourselves on things that don't really cut to the heart of the gospel. I, for example, sometimes measure my effectiveness as a pastor by how many people show up on a Sunday morning to hear me preach. There is nothing wrong with wanting people to come and hear the gospel proclaimed. But that's the visible thing, the part of my work that everybody can see. What if the most important thing I do all week is sit by the bed of someone who is sick or dying and minister with my silent presence? How do I measure that? How does that fit into my definition of "success"?

The chances are good that most of us will not be called to do anything extraordinary today. We are not likely to have large crowds gathering around us, lauding us for how we can instantly change their lives for the better. But we will have the chance to do something sacrificial or at least thoughtful for the sake of others. In some way, we will have the chance to give part of ourselves away. It's not likely to make the evening news, but it might just make the kingdom of God a little more visible.

We should hope for nothing more out of life.

Lord Jesus, help me today to be open to all the big and small ways you are calling me to bear my cross. Help me to be a faithful witness, especially when it does not call attention to me. Thank you for your faithfulness to me in all the circumstances of my life. Amen.

Mark 3:13-19

There is a strange paradox in the story of Jesus. On the one hand, he surrenders fully to the Father's will. That means he gives up the need to control the events happening to him. He allows God's plan for our salvation to unfold accordingly, even though he makes it clear in the Garden of Gethsemane that this is not the plan he would choose if it were up to him. In that regard, Jesus allows himself to be subject to forces beyond his control.

And yet on the other hand, Jesus never becomes a hapless victim of circumstance. He retains his full authority as the Son of God. Just read his pre-crucifixion dialogue with Pontius Pilate in John 18:28-40 and ask yourself which of the two characters seems more in control of the situation. Jesus willingly surrenders to this course of actions because he has the authority to do so.

I think a similar paradox plays out in the lives of believers. On the one hand, we are subject to forces beyond our control. Every day we have to adapt and adjust to circumstances we did not choose. Already this morning I have had to alter my routine because of a sick spouse, a minor car problem, and a last-minute change in who was driving the kid's school carpool. And these are just the minor things! Our lives are pushed and pulled in all sorts of directions, and a big part of the spiritual journey is giving up the illusion that we are in control.

And yet on the other hand, Jesus gives his followers authority— his authority. It says so in today's reading. When Jesus called all the disciples together, he gave them authority, in this case the authority to drive out demons.

If we are in Christ, we have that same authority. We may not be able to control all the circumstances, but we don't have to be hapless victims. We have the authority to drive out the demons of fear, anger, despair, or hatred. The risen Christ gives us authority over the spiritual forces that would love nothing better than to hold us hostage.

I don't know what may be holding you down today. Most likely, some circumstance is unfolding in your life right now that has you stymied. It's true for all of us. It's part of being mortal creatures. But we don't have to yield to a spirit of defeat in the face of those circumstances. We have authority to live as the redeemed children of God.

Lord Jesus, help me to acknowledge and yield to my limitations. You are the Lord of the universe; I am but a creature who lives the blessed life you have given me. But also help me to live fully, creatively, abundantly, and victoriously within those limitations. Reveal to me the demons that are holding me back from the life you have intended. In your Risen Name I pray, Amen.

Mark 3:20-30

Adam and Eve disobeyed God and ate from the tree of the knowledge of good and evil. Ever since that moment, we have struggled with the distinction between right and wrong.

Part of our struggle lies in our ability to recognize evil when it appears. An older seminary professor of mine used to quote a professor from a previous generation who once said, "The devil doesn't always appear in a red suit with a pitchfork." I'm sure we could all fill in the blanks as to how evil approaches us and tempts us.

But equally challenging is our ability to recognize good when it appears. Jesus showed up casting out demons and healing the sick, and the religious leaders accused him of doing it by the power of Satan. Their imaginations were so captive to their preconceived ideas of what God should look like that they were incapable of recognizing when the Lord actually showed up in their midst.

In our world, we've grown suspicious about talk of demons. Such ideas sound too primitive for us. But the unwillingness to recognize spiritual forces at work in our world only further contributes to our ongoing struggle to recognize the hand of God when God acts. We are no less captive in the battle between good and evil than were the Pharisees or Adam and Eve.

A friend received wonderful news yesterday. Despite some peculiar symptoms and the looming fear that his cancer had returned, he learned that he is 100 percent cancer free! How did that happen? Is it merely good luck? Is it the result of a well-functioning health care system? Or is it evidence of an all-powerful God who refuses to abandon us to our own resources?

The way we answer such questions has everything do with our ability to see God at work. Every day—this very day—we are surrounded by indications of God's goodness working through our lives. Every cancer won't be healed, but God will triumph over the spiritual forces of evil—to uplift the downhearted, bring courage to the fearful, and make the weak strong. The greatest mistake we could ever make is to miss it when it happens.

Holy God, open my eyes today to the goodness that you are revealing. I confess that my mind is so captivated by my expectations that I often fail to see you when you come. I trust that even in this world of sin and brokenness and tragedy, you are working to make your kingdom visible to me. Give me the eyes to see it. Through Christ I pray, Amen.

Mark 3:31-35

Few wounds cut deeper than those inflicted on us by our families. I have known plenty of otherwise strong and accomplished adults who still carry in their spirits the pain of broken relationships with parents, siblings, or children.

This is an indication of the family's importance in God's plan for humanity. The family is the single most important socializing agent in a person's life. Families are also hugely important when it comes to evangelism. Most (though clearly not all) of the people in church today came to the faith primarily through the influence of family.

That's why the church needs to come alongside families to encourage and equip them in their ministry to each other. The day before I wrote these words, we dedicated a young child during our worship hour at church. It was a beautiful moment that stood as a sign of the family's and the church's covenant with one another to raise the child in the faith and point him to Jesus.

But let's be clear: the nuclear family is not the end-all, be-all of the kingdom of God. Jesus didn't come into the world just so we can all have 2.5 kids and a white picket fence. As today's reading makes clear, a wider family transcends and even takes precedence over the blood relations that tie us to each other. Jesus says that the true family consists of all those who do the will of the Father.

If you are blessed to have been nurtured into the world through a healthy family unit, then know that your experience among those people is not meant to be an end unto itself. It is meant to point you to the wider and greater reality of God's kingdom family, and to the nurture that only God can provide. If, on the other hand, you have experienced pain or enmity at the hands of family, then know that there is a wider and greater reality of God's kingdom family, and that the nurture you need can only truly come from God. As Psalm 68:5-6a reminds us, "A father to the fatherless, defender of the widows, is God in his holy dwelling. God sets the lonely in families."

That's why the church's greatest ministry to families is the ministry of baptism. In baptism, we welcome new believers into the one true family, the only family that transcends time and place and race, the one family that joins all believers together as children of the one true Father. Through baptism, we all belong to each other, as surely as if we had all been brought home from the same maternity ward.

Despite what others may say, water is thicker than blood.

Lord God, thank you for taking us from our alienation and loneliness and placing us in your family. Help me today to nurture the bonds that I have with my brothers and sisters of the faith. May I never take them for granted. Through Christ, Amen.

Mark 4:1-20

Our first instinct is to view everything in the world through our own eyes. This makes a certain degree of sense. My eyes, after all, are the only ones I inherited at birth. But a part of growing into a mature human being is learning to view the world from a different perspective. How can we arrive at a place where our first question is not, "What does this mean for me?"

It's true even when it comes to Scripture. We read the Bible from a human perspective, and therefore we try to make sense out of what we read from a human perspective. Convinced that ours is the most important vantage point, we try to interpret the text from that place.

But what if the goal of Scripture is to move us out of the center of the story? Take today's reading, for example. We read Jesus' parable of the sower and the soil and immediately think this is a story about us. Jesus describes the different kinds of soils and how each one responds differently to the seed, and our reaction is to try to figure out which kind of soil we represent. Am I the fertile soil, the rocky soil, or the thorny soil? And what do I do if I am not fertile soil? How can I make myself more receptive, more fertile?

That's not necessarily a bad question to ask. We can and should develop disciplines to make our lives more receptive to the word of God. But I don't think this parable is primarily about us. Notice that Jesus doesn't ask or demand that we do anything as a result of this story. That's because this story is first and foremost about the sower, not the soil. The primary actor in this parable is the farmer who sows the seed. He's the one driving the plot. The soil is quite passive.

That's because this parable is not first about us; it is about the lavish and even reckless grace of God. Ask yourself this: What kind of farmer would indiscriminately throw something as precious as seed without first measuring the probabilities and the possibilities of a good crop? You and I would be far more measured and careful and strategic. But this farmer can only be described as wasteful.

This parable describes a God who will stop at nothing to have us. God is willing to "waste" it all for the sake of drawing us to God. What kind of God would waste the seed? It is the same God who will not even spare the Son for our sake.

> *Gracious God, thank you for the fact that you will stop at nothing to have me in your kingdom. Thank you that even when I prove to be unreceptive and unresponsive, you continue to scatter the seed of your love and mercy into my life. Thank you that your actions on my behalf are not based on what I deserve. Thank you for the gift of eternal life through Jesus, in whose name I pray. Amen.*

Mark 4:21-25

"If anyone has ears to hear, let him hear."

These words come in the midst of a series of parables in Mark's Gospel. Parables are a teaching tool meant to illustrate (not explain) the kingdom of God by forming analogies. The kingdom of God is like this or that thing in the natural world, says Jesus. Something that is not obvious is compared to something familiar so that we can begin to see it more clearly. In this way, the parables make the kingdom of God more visible, more accessible.

Yet at the same time, parables have a certain concealing effect. They illustrate the kingdom, but they do it in a way that is not immediately understandable to everyone. The kingdom is like a mustard seed? A farmer who sowed seeds? A landowner who sends a servant to collect the harvest from the tenants? What exactly does this mean? The answer isn't always clear.

That's because the kingdom of God is not exactly like anything else. The kingdom is the realm where God reigns, where God's perfect will is exercised, where everything is exactly like God intends it to be. And nothing about our everyday world matches up with that—not completely. We can catch glimpses of the kingdom. We see little bits of evidence here and there that what God has promised is beginning to come to pass. But not fully. Not yet.

In the meantime, Jesus gives us these parables to stoke our imaginations, to invite us to see the world in ways that transcend our immediate senses. Yes, this world is broken and fallen. Evil happens all around us. And yet at the same time, God is at work redeeming creation. If we look and listen closely enough, we can see it.

Let the one who has ears to hear, hear.

Lord God, help me today to catch a glimpse of your goodness—in the beauty of the creation, in the kindness of others, in the stirrings of hope within me. Most of all, let me see the movement of your Holy Spirit in me, calling me out of my sin and into newness of life. Through Christ, Amen.

Mark 4:26-29

Martin Luther is one of the most significant figures in Western history. His efforts to confront the corruption of the church hierarchy of his day launched the Protestant Reformation and radically altered the political landscape of Western civilization.

How exactly did Luther go about achieving such a remarkable outcome? Listen to his own explanation:

> I simply taught, preached, and wrote God's Word; otherwise I did nothing. And then, while I slept, or drank Wittenberg beer with my Philip [Melanchthon] and my [Nicholaus von] Amsdorf, the Word so greatly weakened the papacy that never a prince or emperor did such damage to it. I did nothing. The Word did it all.[1]

I realize the image of a great church leader sitting around drinking beer with his buddies might seem a bit jarring (just remember that Luther was a man of his times), but Luther's analysis of the events of his day only confirms what Jesus had taught a millennia and a half earlier. The harvest comes not as a result of our careful calculations and strenuous effort but because of the word of God.

As I write these words, we are roughly halfway through the season of Lent, a season that begins with us rubbing ashes on our foreheads as a sign that we are mortal creatures. For all our high achievements in life, we will one day be a pile of ashes. That's why this season calls us to recognize our utter and complete dependence on God. It is only by God's grace that we are saved. Come to think of it, it is only by God's grace that we even exist in the first place.

Luther was right. The Word does it all. And that Word is Jesus.

Lord Jesus, you who are the Word made flesh, forgive me today of my arrogance. Forgive me for assuming that I am at the center of the action. You are the center of gravity. I am only the body in orbit that responds to your pull. May your word take root in my life today. And may that which takes root bear fruit in your time. By your holy name I pray, Amen.

Note

1. Quoted at http://www.patheos.com/blogs/borntoreform/2013/05/my-all-time-favorite-martin-luther-quote/.

Mark 4:30-34

I was in high school when the space shuttle *Challenger* exploded during takeoff, killing everyone on board. It was a shocking and horrifying sight. We had become so accustomed to manned space flight that it seemed almost routine to strap people to a rocket and send them blasting out beyond the earth's atmosphere. We were all reminded that day just how wrong our assumptions had become.

It was later determined that the explosion was caused by a failed gasket on one of the rockets. The temperature the night before the launch had gotten quite low, especially by the standards of central Florida where the launch pad was located. In the freezing air, the rubber gasket had grown hard, preventing it from making a solid seal. Seven astronauts died as a result.

It is tragically ironic. The most sophisticated machine humans had ever built was brought down by a rubber gasket not unlike the ones you can buy at the local hardware store. Never doubt that little things matter.

Jesus says that the kingdom of God is like a mustard seed. Tiny. Insignificant. Easy to ignore. That is, until it sprouts into a full garden plant. In a reverse example of the *Challenger* disaster, the kingdom of God grows with every small thing we do in the name and for the sake of Christ. Every small act of service, every word of encouragement, every unseen sacrifice makes the kingdom more visible.

Most of us will not have the chance to save the world today. But the chances are good that at some point we will have a chance to change the course of someone's day. And who knows? Maybe that also proves to be the point that changes the course of someone's life.

Lord God, I trust that with you at work in the world, even the small things I do matter. Help me today not to neglect the simple opportunities that come my way. Through Christ, Amen.

Mark 4:35-41

This story has always troubled me. On the one hand, everything ends well by the time the story is concluded. The storm is stilled and the disciples land safely on the other side. And just as important, Jesus has been given a chance to demonstrate his awesome power. "Who is this?" ask the disciples. "Even the wind and the waves obey him!" This story seems to be written for the purpose of answering such questions.

But on the other hand, there is that curious detail about Jesus sleeping in the stern of the boat. The disciples are rowing and bailing water as fast as they can, just trying to stay alive, and all the while Jesus is catching a good nap, seemingly oblivious to their struggles. "Teacher, don't you care if we drown?" they ask. It feels like a very honest question.

The implied answer is, "Of course, I care." Jesus does, after all, calm the storm. That fact holds out hope that Jesus may yet choose to calm whatever storm is threatening us. In his time, in his way, he may yet choose to hold out his hand over the turbulent waters of our lives and say, "Be still."

But would you think I am crazy if I said that may not be the most important detail in the story? The key to understanding this story may lie in the fact that Jesus was even in the boat with them at all. He didn't just send the disciples to the other side of the lake; he got in the boat to go there with them. That means he put himself in the path of the same storm that threatened them.

In the Incarnation, God gets as near to us as our own skin. Literally. "The Word became flesh," says John 1:14. There will be times when we wonder or even protest that God is not acting fast enough to respond to the threats and challenges of life. In such moments, we will wonder where God is. But if this story is to be believed, God is right here in the boat with us, allowing himself to be tossed back and forth by the same waves that buffet us.

Lord Jesus, remind me today that you are with me every step of the way. When I grow frustrated that you are not calming the storms of my life quickly enough, open my eyes to see you resting quietly in your Father's care even as the waves toss us back and forth. And teach me to rest there with you. Amen.

Mark 5:1-20

When I was growing up, we would occasionally have missionary speakers come to our church and share stories of their adventures on the mission field. The presentation would always end with some sort of reminder that "God may be calling one of you to the mission field."

That idea used to scare me. I did not want to go to China! For some reason, in those days China seemed to be the place God was calling people. Sure, God had called my family to the town we were living in at the time when my father became pastor of that church, but if God *really* called you, then you went to China. Or maybe it was Africa, or possibly Central America, but China was the real sign of "calledness." At least that's how it seemed in my childhood imagination.

No doubt, God does genuinely call people to such faraway and exotic places. But not always. In today's reading, a man who is healed of an evil spirit wants to leave the place he has been and go with Jesus. It's not hard to blame him, for he has likely earned a bad reputation among the locals. Now that Jesus has healed him, maybe he can go off and get a fresh start somewhere else.

But Jesus says, "No." In this case, Jesus wants the man to stay right where he is. "Go home and tell your family how much the Lord has done for you," Jesus tells him.

I've had the chance now to take a few overseas mission trips. In some ways it is easier to go "over there" and do the Lord's work, because when you are over there you are away from the routine challenges of life back here. Yet the most important work we may do for the kingdom will happen today, right here among the ordinary routines of our lives. We don't have to wait for God to call us to some exotic place to be on mission. It can happen right here where we are.

Blessed are those who are called to stay put.

Lord God, help me to see the routine encounters of my life today as an opportunity to be busy doing the work of your kingdom. Help me to see my family and friends and all the people whose paths I will cross today as my mission field. Through Christ, Amen.

Mark 5:21-43

When you compare the two people in this story, you see an interesting contrast. Jairus was a person of importance. As a synagogue ruler, he held a place of honor and prestige. The woman, on the other hand, was a person of insignificance. Notice that we aren't even given her name. That's because in addition to being a woman (which already marginalized her in her society), she also had a disorder that according to Levitical law made her ritually unclean. For twelve years she had been cut off from participating in the life of her community. She was invisible to everyone but Jesus.

Despite the differences in their stations in life, these characters had two vital things in common. First, they were both up against forces that were bigger than they were. Death and sickness come to all in this world. All the power and prestige in the world cannot insulate us from the vulnerability of being mortal creatures. The president of the United States and the homeless person under the bridge will both eventually succumb to the same fate.

And that leads to the second commonality in this story: they both found their hope in Jesus. They were both willing to cling to the one thing that was greater than what they faced.

We are mortal creatures. We are frail and vulnerable and limited. God created us that way. And yet there is hope for us to live beyond those limitations. His name is Jesus. He may not always heal all our diseases, but he will make us visible to the Father for all eternity.

Holy God, help me today to accept the limitations that come from being your mortal creature. Save me from the foolishness of thinking that I possess within myself the power to overcome the challenges of this life. But also help me to live without fear, knowing that you have already overcome the world. Through Christ, Amen.

Mark 6:1-6a

"And they took offense at him."

Author Phillip Yancey says somewhere that nobody would ever think of crucifying Mr. Rogers or Captain Kangaroo. Someone whose basic agenda is to teach us to be nice, to mind our manners, and to treat people well is generally not going to make us mad enough to want to kill him. So how did Jesus wind up on a cross?

The reason is that Jesus was about far more than just teaching us to be good little boys and girls. Jesus came to offend us with the shocking, death-defeating, sin-conquering, universe-altering, all-consuming grace of God. He came to show us that the path we are on can only lead to death, and that only by dying to ourselves—only by letting go of everything we thought we knew about life—can we find true life.

I am all for good manners. In fact, my wife and I work hard in our home to teach them to our children. And thank God for the wholesome witness of people like Mr. Rogers. But as I write these words, we are a little more than twenty-four hours away from Good Friday, when we will drag Jesus up a hill and nail him to a tree.

Are we willing to be offended by his grace?

Lord Jesus, you are the true source of life. Remind me that only by dying to myself can I embrace the life that you have poured out for me on the cross. Amen.

Mark 6:6b-13

This passage makes us uncomfortable, and not simply for the obvious reason. Yes, Jesus calls his disciples to "travel light" as they go about doing the work of the kingdom. "Take nothing for the journey except a staff," he says. But what about my iPhone and my 50-inch HDTV? Does God really expect me to let go of all that material stuff?

For now I'll let that question fester. The discomfort it causes may not be a bad thing if it forces us to reconsider our posture towards our possessions.

But let's turn our attention to the real source of discomfort in this passage: Jesus gave his followers authority over evil spirits! Why is that discomforting? Because with authority come responsibility and expectations. If Jesus gives his disciples authority over evil spirits, it means he expects them to no longer be hapless victims of those same spirits. And at the very least, it means followers of Christ are expected to have some level of victory over sin.

In some ways, it is much easier to be a victim than to be a victor. If we can convince ourselves that we are only victims to things bigger than us, then we can become passive. We can surrender any kind of moral responsibility for our lives. "It's not my fault," my children sometimes cry when I point out some mistake they've made. "It's not my fault," I often cry when I see area of my life that isn't as it should be. And that means I've pretty much guaranteed that for now I will go on living in the same defeated pattern.

But this is not how Jesus intends it. Yes, we are limited creatures. Our mortality imposes boundaries on what and how much we can do. But if we are born again of the Holy Spirit, we are mortal creatures who just happen to have the living God of the universe dwelling inside us. The risen Christ gives us authority over the evil spirits that want to drag us into their snares. We do not have to be a victim to sin.

So much for my excuses.

Dear Lord, bring to mind today all my tendencies to make excuses for my sin. Show me how I can exercise authority over the evil that is tempting me at every turn. Through Christ, Amen.

Mark 6:14-29

This may sound crazy, but I find myself feeling a slight bit of sympathy for Herod in this story. On the whole Herod is an unsympathetic character. He's murderous and callous. Just read Matthew 2:16. But in this story, Herod at least demonstrates an impulse to preserve John's life. John the Baptist infuriates Herod, for John dares to speak the truth about Herod's moral depravity. And yet something about John also intrigues Herod, so much so that Herod wants to keep him alive.

But then one night at a party, Herod talks himself into a corner. Wanting to impress his guests with his power, he makes a grandiose promise to his stepdaughter. "Ask me for anything you want, and I'll give it to you," he says. Only somebody with the power to make things happen would say such a thing. When the girl asks for John's head on a platter, Herod is stuck. He doesn't want to do it, but if he goes back on his promise he will give people a reason to doubt his resolve and his authority. What's a poor, despotic tyrant to do?

Herod is trapped by his own ego. His is the story of what happens when we choose to worship ourselves. And while perhaps to a less dramatic conclusion, our lives demonstrate a similar pattern. Pride, ego, the self—call it what you will, but it is a power at work within us that wants to preserve itself at all costs. We will lie, cheat, steal, deceive, manipulate, obfuscate, or just outright ignore the truth if it helps us maintain our pride. "Pride goes before destruction," says Proverbs 16:18.

I am not suggesting that the story of Herod is included in the Gospel account merely as some kind of object lesson for us. He is a real character who represents the real effort to oppose what God is doing in Christ. And yet his story does stand as a warning to us. If we choose to put ourselves at the center of our story, it will only lead to destruction and devastation.

Holy God, help me today to have the same spirit within me that was in Christ my Lord, who, even though he was God, chose to lower himself and become a servant of others to the point of death on a cross (see Phil 2:5-8). Help me to get myself out of the way so that I can experience your life flowing through me. Amen.

Mark 6:30-44

"But he answered, 'You give them something to eat.'"

I like to imagine that Jesus said this with a mischievous gleam in his eye. He knew that the need of the moment was overwhelming. There is no way that the disciples had enough resources among them to feed thousands of hungry people. Yet Jesus asks the disciples to feed them anyway. In doing so, he puts them in a situation in which they are forced to recognize their inadequacy.

And yet, by the time the story is ended, everyone has a belly full of food. Even though the disciples could only scrounge up five loaves and two fish, they moved forward with Jesus' command. They began acting as if they did in fact have enough food, and Jesus blessed and multiplied those efforts to meet the need. It turns out that with Jesus on the move, the disciples had everything they needed.

You and I are inadequate. We only have so much of anything. There's only so much money, so much time, so much energy, etc. And that is to say nothing of our sinfulness that drains those precious resources and uses them in ways that do not glorify God. But Jesus calls us to move forward into the world as if there is enough, because with the risen Jesus on the loose among us, there is. He continues to meet us in the midst of our faithful efforts to bless and multiply them for the sake of his kingdom.

As I write these words, there are mission teams from our church family in both Romania and Belize. I am sure that right about now, they are feeling overwhelmed by the level of need they are encountering—needs both physical and spiritual. And yet I am willing to bet that by the time they get home, they will have seen Jesus multiply a few loaves and fish.

Lord Jesus, I confess that I am so inadequate. My sin keeps getting in the way, and I do not always know how to use what you have given me in the best way. But Lord, for the sake of your kingdom, do not hold my sin against me. Take the imperfect and incomplete offerings that I bring today and multiply them. Show to me the simple act of love and sacrifice that I can make on your behalf today, that someone else's life may become more full. In your holy name, Amen.

Mark 6:45-56

This is another one of those miracle stories that modern people like to debate. Come on, now, did Jesus really walk on the water? But to be honest, that's not the part of this story that intrigues me the most. Six chapters into Mark's Gospel, we should by now be used to Jesus doing things that don't fit the normal patterns. If this guy really is who Mark claims he is, then walking on the water shouldn't come as a surprise.

No, the part that causes me the most trouble is at the end of verse 48: "He was about to pass by them . . . ." The disciples are rowing for all they are worth, straining against the wind to get safely to the other side, and Jesus is about to walk right past them. It is only after they cry out that he gets in the boat with them. Why would he not simply come straight to them in their hour of need?

I cannot answer that question with certainty. Throughout Scripture, we see a pattern of God responding in God's own way on God's own time. Only God fully understands these ways. But let me be bold enough to make a suggestion. Perhaps Jesus first intended to pass them by because he already trusted that they would make it safely to the other side. Even though the wind was against them, even though he wasn't in the boat with them, Jesus already knew the outcome of their struggle. The disciples already had the ability to row that boat to the shore.

We think of the Bible as a call for us to have faith in God, which it is. But what if Scripture is also making the bold claim that God has a certain amount of faith in us? The Incarnation is the story of a God who works in concert with humanity, calling us into partnership in the work to redeem the world. "For we are God's fellow workers," says Paul in 1 Corinthians 3:9.

Make no mistake. We are sinners. In our own right, we have nothing good in us. We are saved by Christ's merits, not by ours. And yet God sees something in us worth redeeming. For all our brokenness God sees something usable, and so God has entrusted the work of the kingdom into our hands. And God knows that the struggle to which we are called will one day end well.

Holy God, I want you to crawl into this boat and calms the seas. But for now you have seen fit to allow me to continue rowing into the wind. Give me the faith to trust that the task to which you have called me is worth the effort, and that in your time you will see to it that I land safely on the other side. Through Christ I pray, Amen.

Mark 7:1-23

I once heard another preacher tell about an advertisement he saw. It was a brochure for a private Christian school that hailed itself as being located "seventeen miles from the nearest known source of sin."

I can appreciate the effort that school was making to withdraw itself from the distractions and temptations of the world around us. There is no denying that the world is filled with evil and darkness, and we have to be careful what we allow into our spirits. Much like food, the more moral junk we let in, the unhealthier our souls become.

But Jesus warns us against the fallacy of thinking that the real source of sin is located "out there." That's what the Pharisees believed. If they could only cut themselves loose from the uncleanness of the world around them, they would be safe. Not so, says Jesus. It is not what comes into us that makes us unclean; it is what comes out of us.

The real source of sin is not out there in the world. It is in *here*, in the rebellious spirit that lives within me. If there were no sinful nature already residing in me, then it wouldn't matter what kind of temptation I encountered in the world. There would be nothing within me for it to trigger. But because a sinful nature lives in me, I can cut myself off from all the outside influences and still end up adrift in darkness.

The antidote to that darkness is not to withdraw from the contaminating influence of the world, for that would require us to withdraw from the very world Jesus died to save. The antidote is to allow the purifying wind of the Holy Spirit to blow through my life. Only by being cleansed within can I be truly clean.

Lord Jesus, you ate with sinners and fellowshipped with prostitutes, yet you remained fully without sin. Thank you that you have offered the same holiness up on my behalf. Save me from self-righteousness, and help me to embrace the world with the same humble love that is in you. Amen.

Mark 7:24-30

We now live across the street from the foot of Tinker Mountain, so I have started reading Annie Dillard's Pulitzer Prize-winning *Pilgrim at Tinker Creek*. Early in the book, she describes how, as a kid, she hid pennies in conspicuous places in hopes that others would find them. She found it a great thrill to think that someone would be so fortuitous as to stumble across such an unexpected and unearned gift!

Of course, as we grow up we lose any sense of appreciation for the value of a penny, whether it is earned or found. Few people are likely to get excited over discovering something that seems so meaningless. But Dillard writes that it is shameful that we lose a sense of our utter poverty to the point that we are no longer able feel joy in finding a penny. The world has so many pennies to offer us. Every day we are surrounded by unexpected and undeserved acts of grace and beauty if only we are open to them.

In Mark 7, Jesus has a conversation with a Syrophoenician woman. That's a fancy way of saying she wasn't Jewish. She didn't belong to God's covenant people, a fact that Jesus illustrates with his somewhat obscure statement about tossing the children's bread to dogs. In other words, the gifts of God are for Israel first, and only then for the Gentiles.

Yes, says the woman, but all I need is a few crumbs falling from the table and I will be satisfied. In other words, even the slightest encounter with grace will be more than enough to meet her need.

Today there are pennies lying all around, waiting to be found. Little bits of God's grace are available in abundant supply for those who have the eyes to see them and the hands to pick them up. It's almost like someone put that penny there on purpose, just hoping I would find it!

O God, make me open to the indications of your beauty that are available all around me. Help me to trust that even the slightest encounter with your grace will be enough to sustain me in my need. Through Christ I pray, Amen.

Mark 7:31-37

Sarah Churman was born severely hearing impaired. While not completely deaf, the mother of two had never heard her daughters' voices. She'd never heard her husband's voice. She'd never even heard her own voice. But then at age twenty-nine she underwent surgery to receive a special implant. A now virally popular YouTube video shows what happened when the device was turned on for the first time. Sarah Churman broke down and wept. (If you can get to a computer, go to YouTube and enter her name in the search bar. The video will bring a few tears to your eyes as well!) She's written a book about her experience titled *Powered On: The Sounds I Choose to Hear and the Noise I Don't.*

I've been blessed with good hearing all my life, so it is hard for me to understand what it is like to go from deafness to clear sound in an instant. That said, I think that sudden transition is a good illustration of what grace is all about. If you've lived in a sound vacuum all your life, then there is absolutely no reason to expect that the future will hold out anything different for you. Experience shows that what happened yesterday is usually a good predictor of what will happen tomorrow. And I am not just talking about issues of physical health and wellness. Relationships, emotions, finances, the spiritual quest— no matter the issue, what has been tends to determine what will be.

But then one day Jesus sticks his fingers in a man's ears and spits, and for the first time in his life a man who had only known silence found the world filled with wonderful sound.

Grace unfolds in our lives at different speeds. Sometimes it brings about a sudden, dramatic, even miraculous change. Other times the healing comes gradually, maybe even after a long period of struggle. Either way, God's grace means that the future is not bound by the past. No matter what our past struggles have been, life is still filled with glorious possibility.

Just ask Sarah Churman.

Lord Jesus, help me today to hear you speaking into my life the same words you spoke into the deaf man's ears long ago: "Ephphatha! Be opened!" Amen.

Mark 8:1-13

The story is told of a man whose house was caught in a terrible flood. As the waters rose, he climbed out on the roof. Over the next few hours, two boats and a helicopter came by, each offering to carry the man to safety. He politely refused each offer, declaring that he was trusting God to save him. Eventually, the waters rose higher and swept him away to his death. When he arrived in heaven, he asked St. Peter why God had not come to save him. St. Peter responded, "You idiot, we sent you two boats and a helicopter! What more did you want?"

Sometimes we are looking for a miraculous sign when God is right in front of us.

The Pharisees came to Jesus demanding a miraculous sign, yet Jesus had just fed four thousand people with seven loaves of bread. How much more of a sign did they need?

Of course, we know from the text that the Pharisees had an ulterior motive. They weren't asking out of a genuine desire to see God; they were asking out of a desire to test and trap Jesus. It didn't matter if Jesus had fed twenty thousand people with three rocks and a leather sandal, for the Pharisees were not willing even to consider the possibility of looking at Jesus through the eyes of faith. Because skepticism was their starting point, skepticism was the only place they could land.

The fact is that Jesus feeds billions of hungry people every day. I know, because I am one of them. And so are you. The fact that our food comes to us through the more obvious channels of grocery stores and restaurants makes it no less amazing that God engineered the world in such a way that it produces more than enough food to satisfy every stomach. Politicians and pundits may say that is the result of a well-functioning economy. The Bible says it is a function of God's generosity.

Today our world will be filled with miraculous signs. The sun will rise, the rivers will run, the rains will fall, the wind will blow, and the human ability for creative work and productivity will play itself out. In short, all the normal events necessary to sustain human life will continue to be poured out on us. Will we see these gifts for what they are?

Holy God, thank you that you continue to satisfy the hungry, befriend the lonely, care for the sick, and provide for even the birds of the field. Help me today to recognize the signs of your continued care and abundance. Through Christ, Amen.

Mark 8:14-21

I was riding in a car with a friend when we passed a field of cows. I noticed that many of the cows were lying down. Trying to recall some bit of popular wisdom I had heard earlier in my life, I asked my friend, "What does it mean when cows are lying down?"

"I always just thought it meant they were tired!" he said.

Sometimes things really are as simple as they seem.

But sometimes they are not. Jesus warns the disciples about what he called "the yeast of the Pharisees." The disciples' minds were still reeling from the miraculous feeding they had just witnessed and the conflict with the Pharisees that had ensued. So they figured that Jesus' words could only be about literal bread.

But Jesus had something much more important in mind. He was calling the disciples to beware of the mindset of skepticism and bitterness that characterized the Pharisees' interactions with Jesus. Such a mindset is like yeast. Give yeast enough time, and it will leaven the entire batch of dough. Allow enough cynicism into your thoughts, and it will eventually color your entire worldview.

This story is a reminder that there is more going on in life than what we take in with our immediate senses. We have to learn to view life through the eyes of faith. Life with God is rich and layered and nuanced. That doesn't mean that God is trying to confuse us. God's desire is to be known to us. It does mean that every event, every conversation, every moment is infused with a deeper meaning. God never tires of trying to reveal holy purposes to us.

This past Sunday, our congregation shared the Lord's Supper. As I held up the bread and repeated the words of institution—"This is my body, which is for you; do this in remembrance of me"—we were all reminded that sometimes bread is more than bread.

Holy God, help me to see the sacredness of each moment of my life today. Save me from a one-dimensional view of life so that I might perceive the richness and beauty of the truth you are trying to reveal to me. Most of all, help me to see that Jesus is the bread of life and the fullness of your truth. Through Christ, Amen.

Mark 8:22-26

This is the only story I recall in which Jesus has to make two attempts at a miracle. He rubs spittle and mud on a blind man's eyes once and gets partial success. The eyes start letting in light for the first time, but the vision isn't clear. "I see people," the man said, "but they look like trees walking around." Jesus has to touch the man's eyes a second time in order for the man to see truly as he should.

What happened? Did Jesus miss the mark the first time? Did he not rub enough spit into the mud? Did he misjudge the severity of the man's blindness?

Hardly. This story is given to us to make a point—a point that has little to do with the acuity of our visual system. There is seeing, and then there is seeing. Just because our eyes are letting light into our visual cortex does not mean that we are truly perceiving things accurately. What we see is affected by so many things going on within us—our habits and patterns, our preconceived ideas, our immediate needs, the latest crisis to consume our energies, and more. These things can move us toward or away from seeing the world as God does, depending on how we respond to them.

Most mornings it is my job to get my daughters out of bed and delivered to school. What do I see when I first walk into their room (aside from the clutter)? Do I see an opportunity to bless and encourage two young people as they prepare to meet the challenges of a new day? Or do I see only another task to perform and hurdle to clear before I can get on with my responsibilities?

There is seeing, and then there is seeing.

Father God, I confess that I tend to see what I want to see. I see the things that confirm my preconceived notions about the world. I see the things that can help me get what I want out of life. But you see the world differently. You see the world as it truly is—broken by sin and marred by suffering and yet brimming over with beauty and goodness and generosity. Help me today to see my world with your eyes. Help me to see the people around me not as means to an end but as objects of your divine love. Help me to see my failures as an opportunity to learn and grow. Help me to see the obstacles as occasions for relying on your grace. Help me to see life itself as a gift to be received and not as a right to be asserted. Give me the mind of Christ. Amen.

Mark 8:27-30

It is a demonstrable fact that no figure in history has generated more interest, curiosity, and debate than Jesus of Nazareth. It's not only true of people who believe in him; even nonbelievers must acknowledge the central role that his name and legacy have played in the unfolding of human history.

In recent years there has been great interest among a certain group of scholars in what is known as the "historical Jesus." Behind this move is the assumption that the Jesus presented to us in Scripture is the result of layers of tradition and even legend that are piled on top of the actual person. Groups like the Jesus Seminar have attempted to deconstruct the "alleged" sayings of Jesus in an effort to distinguish between what the real Jesus actually said and what has only been attributed to him over time. As a professor of mine once put it, when a group of white, middle-class scholars gets together for something like this, you end up with a Jesus who strangely resembles a white, middle-class scholar!

We can debate and argue over Jesus all we want. We can read, ponder, accept, or reject certain strains of scholarship associated with his name. We can believe what the Scriptures say about him or reject them in favor of some other truth claims. But at the end of the day, every single one of us must decide what we are going to do with Jesus. It is a personal choice we must each make, and even not deciding is deciding.

Jesus asked the disciples what people were saying about him. The disciples responded with the latest survey data. "Focus groups are responding well to your miracles," they say. "Your message is working well among single parents aged 18-28, but you're not polling so well among college-educated folks in the suburbs."

"Yes," Jesus said, "but what about you. Who do you say I am?" Everything turns on that question. Who do you say I am?

Today, whether we realize it or not, we will answer that question. The things we say and do will reveal our response. Today, who will we say Jesus is? A curious figure of history? An interesting subject of debate? Or Lord of the universe?

Lord Jesus, make me mindful today of who you are. In every-thing I say and do, may I be aware of you. Be the Lord of my life today. In your name I pray, Amen.

Mark 8:31–9:1

The story of Jesus begins to a make an ominous turn with today's reading. Up until now, Jesus' ministry has been mostly about things that people can celebrate. Jesus has healed the sick, opened the eyes of the blind, fed the hungry, and generally said and done things that could win the approval of people. (There was that dark stain on the story when John the Baptist got beheaded, but you can almost be convinced to write that off as the delusional behavior of a despotic Herod.)

And then comes this: "The Son of Man must suffer many things . . . and . . . he must be killed." And "If anyone would come after me, he must deny himself and take up his cross and follow me."

The word "must" is what grabs my attention. The suffering that Jesus undergoes, and the suffering love to which he calls his followers, is not an accident or coincidence. It is the design of the Father. God sent Jesus into the world to save not in spite of the suffering he faced but through that suffering. Suffering love is the mechanism through which God acts to redeem us, and it is the way in which those who follow are called to witness to that redemption.

The Christian faith is often presented as though it is the answer to every question and the solution to every problem. Love Jesus and you will be blessed with health and happiness, we are told. I don't think Jesus necessarily has anything against health and happiness, but I don't see how health and happiness can be the primary agenda of a man who talks about how he must go to the cross and how we must follow him there.

Today we will be confronted with opportunities to enter into the world's suffering—both our own and that of others. The world tells us to find a way around it. But Jesus walks right into the midst of it and then invites us to follow him there.

Lord Jesus, help me to love others in the way you have loved me. Show me how to embrace the sadness and suffering of others as a witness to your redeeming love. Show me the way of the sacrificial life today. Through Christ, Amen.

Mark 9:2-13

It is an obvious fact that you cannot look directly at the sun. Expose your eyes to that much intense light for more than a fraction of a second, and you can do permanent damage. You can even go blind. And yet it is also an obvious fact that were it not for the sun's intensity, life on Earth wouldn't be possible. We need that much light and heat to sustain the cycles of energy that keep us alive.

Interesting. That which keeps us alive also has the ability to hurt us, even kill us.

The disciples go with Jesus to a mountaintop where he is "transfigured" before them. There is no clear or obvious natural equivalent by which to make sense of that word. Something beyond normal experience is happening. For a moment, the veil of Jesus' flesh is pulled back and the fullness of his divine glory shines through. And the light and heat are so intense that the disciples can barely stand to look directly at their Lord.

Notice how their comments seem to steer attention away from what has happened. They've just witnessed something indescribable, and their response is to try to engage Jesus in a theological discussion. "So tell us about Elijah," they say. They almost can't handle the fullness of what has happened, so they try to come at it indirectly. The sense of the story is "This is too much for us. Let's talk about things that we can understand." It is as though the disciples are giving Jesus a sideways glance in fear that a direct gaze would blind them.

Imagine you and a friend witness something truly amazing. Whatever it is, it is beyond description. And your friend turns to you and says, "So, did you see that game last night?" He doesn't know what to think about what has happened, so he chooses instead to focus on something that makes sense to him.

But notice that Jesus doesn't fault the disciples for their indirect approach. For one thing, their inquisitiveness is genuine. Jesus welcomes honest questions. But more important, he knows this is how it is with God's glory. It is too much for us to take directly. Exposed to the fullness of God's holiness and righteousness, we would melt. God dwells in unapproachable light, according to 1 Timothy 6:16.

And yet God has taken all that glory and intensity and has stuffed it into human flesh. The Son is the radiance of God's glory and the exact representation of God's being (Heb 1:3). We may not be able to look directly at the Father, but we don't need to.

We can look directly at the Son.

Lord Jesus, you are the perfect representation of the fullness of God. Help me today to yield before your greatness and your glory. Help me to stand in awe of who you are and what you have done. Help me not to avert may gaze towards lesser things but to keep my eyes fixed firmly on you. You alone are my hope and my salvation. Amen.

Mark 9:14-32

"I do believe; help me overcome my unbelief."

We live in an age that lauds doubt as the highest of all possible virtues. In our quest for personal autonomy, we have created the ideal of the modern mind as one that is aloof, uncommitted, and never swayed by the silly traditions of the past. The path to true freedom, we are told, is to question everything. Don't believe anything until you have tested it for yourself and found it to be true to your own experience.

To be sure, authentic questioning is an important vehicle for learning and growth in any field of life. No one can doubt, for example, the power of the scientific method—a method that necessarily involves questioning and exploring—to lead us to amazing discoveries and advancements in knowledge.

But even the scientific method begins with a basic unquestioned assumption that can never be proven, only accepted. It is the assumption that there is such a thing as objective reality, and that if we ask the right questions we can come to know more of that reality. Without that beginning point, all technological progress would grind to a halt. Why go into a laboratory to ask questions if you don't think there is an answer to be found?

The same principle applies to the spiritual life. It is fine and good to ask questions. If God really is who we say God is, then God is big enough to handle it. God has nothing to hide and nothing for which to apologize. So ask away! But what is our motive? Are we asking and seeking because we genuinely want to know more and go deeper, or is our asking only a way to avoid the claims of Truth on our lives?

Doubt is an inevitable part of life. Every one of us will at some point question what we claim to believe. If you happen to be at a place right now where doubt is your constant companion, then know that God does not begrudge you for that. But is our doubt in service to the larger goal of knowing more about who God is, or is our doubt only a way to avoid God?

Today's Scripture lesson is a story of faith and doubt: the faith to trust in God even as doubt compels us to know more about why we should. We would do well to understand that the two have everything to do with each other.

Father God, I believe, even as I struggle with unbelief. Help me offer up to you whatever level of incomplete faith I find stirring in my soul today. And help me to offer up even my unbelief as part of my quest to know you more. Through Christ, Amen.

Mark 9:33-37

Between the crises in Ukraine and South Sudan, the secretary of state has a full plate these days. Whenever the secretary visits such a place, it is his or her job not only to seek a resolution to the problem but also to do so representing the interests of the United States. To that end, the secretary of state speaks with the full authority of the president. The way our system of government is set up, the secretary fully represents the president in matters of foreign policy. Those who speak to the secretary can have confidence that they are indirectly speaking to the president.

"Whoever welcomes me does not welcome me but the one who sent me," Jesus says. Jesus is the full representation of the Father. Far beyond the case with the secretary of state, it is not *as if* those who speak to Jesus are speaking to God; they *are* speaking to God. When we look at Jesus, we are looking at exactly who God is. Jesus is the perfect and best look we will ever have at who God is and what God is like.

And what is God like? He is like a man who will kneel down and take a small child into his arms. The infinite God of the universe welcomes the small and helpless into his presence. The ancient world was a hostile place for kids. Until children were old enough to work the fields or earn an income, they were only a liability to families. There was no department of child welfare to look out for them. And these are the ones God welcomes.

"If anyone wants to be first, he must be the very last, the servant of all," Jesus said. This is exactly what Jesus did; he was the servant of all. And as Jesus has done, so has the Father.

Holy Father, thank you for welcoming me into your presence. Thank you that through Christ you stooped to my level to show me your grace. Save me from the pride of thinking that my status as your child is rooted in me or what I have done. And help me to welcome others as you have welcomed me. Through Christ, Amen.

Mark 9:38-41

"I'm not a religious person, but I believe that we should do good in the world." I've heard such comments more times than I can count. So have you. On the surface it is a nice sentiment. Who can argue with the desire to do good in the world?

Today's reading even seems to support such a thought. Confronted with someone who wasn't necessarily a member of his official team, Jesus told the disciples to leave him alone. After all, the guy was doing good for people. Combine this with the fact that Jesus seemed at times to demonstrate a dislike for the organized religious strictures of his day, and you get the idea that Jesus isn't too concerned with religion. Just get out there and do some good, and don't worry about all that silly doctrine.

"Whoever is not against us is for us," says Christ.

But there is an interesting twist in the final verse of this passage. We expect Jesus to say something along the lines of, "Whoever gives a cup of water to others will not lose his reward." In other words, "Whoever is making an earnest effort to be a good person has already earned my approval." But that's not exactly what he says. Remember that Jesus is speaking directly to his disciples when he says, "Anyone who gives you a cup of water in my name because you belong to Christ will certainly not lose his reward."

This isn't a passage about some generalized spirit of good in the world. This is a passage of reassurance that those who have committed themselves to the work of Christ will find sources of support and encouragement and nourishment as they go about their work. Our provisions may not always come from the expected and approved channels of the organized church. But they will come. They may come from unlikely sources. Just read the story of the Good Samaritan in Luke 10.

You've probably heard the old saying that beggars can't be choosers. In other words, when we are in desperate need, we do not have the luxury of examining the aid that comes our way.

And we are all beggars before God.

Holy God, help me today not to spurn or reject your help just because it comes to me from an unlikely source. Help me instead to receive every act of kindness and generosity as a sign of your unyielding sustenance of my life. Through Christ, Amen.

Mark 9:42-50

The spiritual writer Richard Rohr has a book titled *The Spirituality of Subtraction*, in which his basic point is that authentic spirituality is about letting go of things. For most of us, our lives are full and over-crowded. We have more possessions, more obligations, more events, and more choices than we know what to do with. (Seriously, how many gears does a mountain bike really need?) And on top of that, we want to add some "spirituality" as a way of hopefully making sense of it all.

But true spirituality is not about stuffing something else into an already overbooked day planner. Spirituality is about letting go, paring down, and stripping away what is nonessential so that we are left with room to breathe in authentic truth.

Jesus is even more jarring. True spirituality is not just about letting go; it is about amputation! If your arm causes you to sin, cut it off. If your eye causes you to sin, gouge it out. Better to be a one-eyed, one-armed inhabitant of the kingdom than to be able-bodied in hell!

If I am going to be an authentic disciple, then I've got to be willing to cut things out of my life that would keep me separated from Jesus and from the things he wants from me. I can't be parked for three hours every night in front of my HDTV (complete with surround sound!) and still give my family the time and attention I should. I can't spend all my money on frivolous things that make me happy and still live a life of generosity towards others. I can't be careless and cynical with my tongue and still hope to bless others the way I have been called to do. Something has to go in order to make room for something else.

What do we need to strip away or cut out today?

Lord Jesus, you are unapologetic and unwavering in your demand to have all of me, and yet I want to hold back just a little bit for myself. Help me today to let go of the things that cause me to sin. Give me the grace to yield myself fully to the things and people that matter to you. Help me to be salty. In your name I pray, Amen.

Mark 10:1-12

My daughters and I have a running debate about the cleanliness of their rooms. I will routinely ask them to go clean up a particular mess they have made, and they will quickly return claiming to have completed the task. Of course, when I go to inspect, I usually find that their work doesn't quite match up to my standard.

The problem (beyond my self-diagnosed OCD!) is that in their childish way of thinking, they have met the basic obligation I placed on them. I asked them to clean up a certain mess, and they did just that. But that is all they did. Instead of asking, "What would make my room look really clean?" or "What would really please Dear Old Dad?" they instead ask, "What is the bare minimum I can do to meet the basic requirements?" It is a way of thinking that says, "You asked me to do something and I did it. Now I can move on to the next thing."

On the whole, my daughters are respectful and obedient, and in this case they can be excused for thinking like children, because they are. But as adults we bring the same basic thought patterns into our spiritual lives. If religion is about the rules, then what is the basic minimum requirement I must meet in order to be safe? How can I meet my duty to God so that I can move on with my life?

That way of thinking plays into the Pharisees' question about divorce in today's reading. If anybody was into rules, it was these guys. So, Jesus, what do the rules say? Can a man leave his wife or not?

As he often does, Jesus tries to show them that the very premise of the question is misguided. Marriage, like the spiritual life as a whole, is not about keeping the rules. It is about losing oneself in a relationship of trust and mutual respect. The only reason there are rules is because of our sinful habit of holding back on that trust. Our hearts are hard, and so God has given us rules to protect others from our hardness.

But the question to ask is not, "What is the minimum obligation I must meet to fulfill my duties?" That's a rather unexciting way to live. The better question is, "How can I best please my spouse? How can I best serve my neighbor? How can I best lose myself in a posture of trust and joy?"

How can I best please my God? If we can get the answer to that question right, then the need for divorce will be rare indeed.

Lord God, help me today to see all my relationships in the light of what best pleases you. Save me from treating the people in my life as obligations to be met. Help me instead to see them as opportunities to know even more of your heart for this world. Through Christ, Amen.

Mark 10:13-16

On a recent morning, my second-grade daughter announced that she was taking her Bible to school. She explained that her teacher likes for them to read something if they finish their work ahead of others. "Maybe I can use that time to read my Bible," she said as she stuffed it in her book bag.

It is interesting to consider what her motivation might be for such a thing. Her mother and I have never suggested that she take her Bible to school, so she certainly wasn't doing it to please us. And at seven years of age, she has little concept of the culture wars that are spinning around us. I seriously doubt she was taking her Bible in protest that her public school day doesn't begin with a chapel service. This was not about making a statement or earning a reward.

No, she was taking her Bible simply because she has a childlike wonder about the things of God. She may not yet understand everything she reads on those pages, but she's had just enough experience with God that she thinks God is really cool! She approaches God with the same joy and abandon she has when she's wrestling with our golden retriever or jumping in a pile of leaves I just raked.

I think that is the attitude Jesus is trying to convey in today's reading. When he tells us to receive the kingdom of God like a little child, he is not calling us to be immature in our thinking and acting. In fact, later in the New Testament the Apostle Paul calls us to put childish ways behind us as we grow up in the Lord (1 Cor 13:11).

Jesus is calling us once again to be willing to approach God with the kind of joy and simple trust that a child demonstrates. When a child runs to his mother's arms at the end of the school day, he is not analyzing or critiquing or strategizing or manipulating. He is not thinking about what this act will produce or how it will benefit him in the long run. He is simply celebrating the joy of being with someone he loves and trusts, someone he knows always has his best interests at heart.

When you think about it, that is all God has ever wanted from us.

Holy God, help me to be like a child before you today. Show me again the joy of simply trusting in your goodness and celebrating your presence. And if necessary, give me a pile of leaves to jump in! Through Christ, Amen.

Mark 10:17-31

You may have heard the story of how some African hunters catch a monkey. They place food in something with a small opening at one end, such as a jar or a hollowed-out coconut. Eventually a monkey comes along and reaches his hand into the jar to retrieve the food, which means that his hand is now in a fist. But the fist won't fit back through the narrow opening of the jar. The monkey is now stuck. And the hunter captures his prey.

The ironic thing is that all the monkey has to do is let go of the food. The open hand would easily fit back out of the jar just as it first fit into the jar, and the monkey would be free, but in his panic he can't think clearly enough to realize that. Either that, or he simply is not willing to part with the banana slice or the peanuts that he is now convinced belong to him. (And yes, you can go to YouTube and actually see this happen!)

In today's passage, a rich man asks Jesus how he can know more of the kind of life Jesus is offering. After some theological discussion, Jesus tells him that the answer is really quite simple. Just go and sell everything you have! And then we read that the man went away sad, because he had great wealth.

Our first reaction to this story is to go on the defensive or engage in a theological debate. Surely Jesus doesn't ask this of all his followers, does he? Do I have to get rid of my car and my clothes and my golf clubs and my new iPad? How much is enough and how much is too much?

But before we start compiling a list of what we think we are allowed to have and what we are forbidden to have (an almost impossible task), let's think about the poor monkey. Freedom is his if only he will let go of the banana! And yet his insistence on having it for himself leads to his death.

The man in today's story is like that monkey. And so are we. We've got our hand stuck in the jar and we aren't willing to let go of what has us trapped. Eventually the life and vitality is drained out of us. Satan has his prey.

Holy God, show me today the things that have me trapped. The possessions, the habits, the unhealthy relationships, the negative thoughts—all that would keep me from experiencing the fullness of life for which you created me. Through Christ, Amen.

Mark 10:32-34

As a preacher, I feel a certain pressure every week to offer people something that is practical and relevant to their lives. After all, we in the church like to portray Jesus as the answer to every question and the solution to every problem. Besides, if people are going to bother to show up for church this week, then I need to demonstrate to them that it is worth their effort. Otherwise they may choose to spend next Sunday at home or at their grandkid's soccer tournament. So I offer three steps or four principles or five foolproof strategies from Jesus to improve your life. Oprah's got nothing on me!

Maybe that's why, in a decade and a half of preaching, I don't recall ever once preaching on this passage of Scripture. On the way to Jerusalem, Jesus takes his disciples aside and repeats to them something he already said once before. "Look, guys, soon enough I am going to be arrested, mocked, tortured, and killed. And then three days later I am going to rise again." That's it. We aren't told what the disciples or we are supposed to do with that information. There are no commands, no suggestions, and no advice. No strategies for happier living here.

Which takes us right to the heart of the gospel. The Bible has plenty of practical guidance on a wide range of subjects, but the Bible is not first and foremost a guidebook for how to get along better in life. There is nothing "practical" about a bleeding Jew hanging from a cross. The crucifixion is an image of helplessness and weakness. And yet the Bible never lets us get away from it. It even goes so far as to proclaim that the crucifixion is at the heart of the very meaning of life itself.

In the first analysis, there's not much we can do about it, and maybe that is the point. The word "gospel" does not mean good advice. It means good news. And the good news is that Jesus has done what only he can do. He has saved us. And he did so long before we had the good sense ask for it, much less demonstrate our worthiness of it.

That said, there is one thing we can do—and it is the only thing we can do. We can give ourselves totally and completely to him in joy and gratitude.

Holy God, no words can fully express the mystery of what you have done for me. You have taken my place, paid my penalty, and sealed my destiny. And you did it entirely because of who you are. Help me to trust that your love for me is without end and without measure. Through Christ, Amen.

Mark 10:35-45

One of my daughter's friends was visiting with her in the church I pastored at the time. She looked around the recently renovated lobby, taking in the new ceramic-tile floors and the flat-screen monitors on the wall. Knowing that I was the pastor, she looked at me and said, "Wow, is all of this yours?"

It was a comical moment, yet it revealed an assumption that underlies much of our thinking even after we become adults. We are led to believe that to be in a position of leadership is to be in a place of power, prestige, or possession. Because I was the pastor—the visible leader—it must mean that all this was "mine." (Just for the record, I answered her question with an emphatic "no!")

In today's reading, Jesus chastises the disciples for wanting to assume places of power and prestige. They wanted others to see them and respect them and honor them. They wanted to be known for the glory of their role. But Jesus says that among his followers, it is not to be that way. Those who will come after him must be willing to be servants of others. In an ironic twist of logic, Jesus says that those who want to be great will make themselves the least.

Maybe that's why Jesus never spent time in the places of power in his day. He avoided cultural centers, choosing to spend his time out in the forgotten backwaters of Israel, in the places where the people of no repute or prestige lived. He did eventually go to Jerusalem, but the only reason he went there was to die.

All of us lead someone. Our families, our neighbors, our coworkers—somebody somewhere is influenced by us. By definition, that makes us leaders. And according to Jesus, one who leads is one who serves.

Holy God, show me whom you want me to serve today. Help me to be selfless in my dealings with others. Help me to put their needs ahead of mine. And help me to understand what true greatness looks like in your kingdom. Through Christ, Amen.

Mark 10:46-52

"Cheer up! On your feet! He's calling you!"

When someone calls your name, what do you do? My guess is that you stop whatever you are doing and look for the source of the voice. It doesn't matter if you are in a crowded mall surrounded by strangers, or in the living room of your home with only a handful of family members near, the sound of someone calling your name has an almost irresistible pull on you. You have been issued a summons that you cannot ignore.

When Jesus tells the crowd that he wants to speak to Bartimaeus, they say to the blind man, "Good news! He's calling you!" As readers of the story, we already know the eventual outcome; Bartimaeus will receive his sight. But at the moment, none of the characters in the original story can know that. All they know is that Jesus is calling this man whom almost everyone else ignores. And that alone is sufficient cause for cheer and encouragement.

By this point in Mark's Gospel, we are used to Jesus healing the sick and opening the eyes of the blind. So far Jesus has not encountered a single need that he has not met. But there has got to be more to the good news of the gospel than that. While Jesus healed every sick person he met, he did not meet every sick person. If the only thing we can hope for is the occasional miraculous healing, then the gospel will often leave us disappointed.

The first source of encouragement in this story is that Jesus called Bartimaeus. A useless beggar on the street, he likely received almost no attention from anyone else. But Jesus called him. And that call was enough to get old Bartimaeus up on his feet and moving.

Just as he has done with every other follower, Jesus calls us. By name. He has something for us, and he calls us to him that he might give it to us. The question is whether we hear the call and respond. Do we allow his call to be that irresistible pull, or do we let his voice be drowned out by all the others who are also calling us?

No matter where life finds us today, Jesus is not through with us. He still has something for us. The words of this passage still ring out, saying, "Cheer up! On your feet! He's calling you!"

Holy God, help me today to hear your voice. As the child hears his mother, as the sheep hears his shepherd, help me to recognize the distinctive sound of you calling me. Through Christ, Amen.

Mark 11:1-11

We humans are an ambitious race. There are so many things we want to accomplish in life. From our earliest days, we are taught that there is nothing we cannot do if we only put our minds to it and work hard.

That mindset has rewarded us. By channeling our God-given creative powers, we have done amazing things—from building the great pyramids to putting a man on the moon to curing diseases to creating great works of art and music. The human spirit is alive and strong.

But there is one thing we will never be able to do, no matter how hard we work or how deeply we strive. And this one thing that we cannot do for ourselves is the one thing we most deeply need. You and I will never be able to atone for our sin. No amount of effort or good will can cover the fact that we have broken our relationship with our Creator. It is our natural state to be at enmity with God, and there is nothing we can do about it.

But God can, and God has.

In today's reading, we watch Jesus march into Jerusalem. For the moment there is an air of celebration. Jesus is coming into the holy city to celebrate the Passover with his people. But as the cheers erupt, there are storm clouds gathering on the horizon. Within a few days, this same Jesus will be dead, the victim of a ruthless plot by those who are convinced that they are doing God's will.

Yet here is the irony. While those who would kill him thought they were putting an end to him, it turns out that through the painful events of his betrayal, arrest, conviction, and death, Jesus fulfills the Father's plan to rescue us from sin and death and restore us to a right relationship with him. Jesus goes forth into Jerusalem to do for us what we cannot do for ourselves.

And because of that, we are set free.

Holy God, help me to stand in awe of what you have accomplished on my behalf. Help me to recognize the price of my sin, which you were willing to pay. And help me add my voice to those who cry, "Hosanna! Blessed is he who comes in the name of the Lord!"

Mark 11:12-19

A traveling music group came to perform at a church I once pastored. They wanted to set up a table to sell merchandise—mostly CD recordings—when their concert was over. But they insisted that the table not be anywhere in the sanctuary. An adjacent hallway was as near as they would put it.

Behind that decision was this passage. Jesus came into the temple one day and turned over the tables of the money changers and drove out those selling doves. The standard interpretation has been that Jesus doesn't like business being transacted in the holy place.

But there is something much deeper going on here. Our standard readings notwithstanding, these merchants were there to provide important practical resources for traveling pilgrims to use in making offerings and sacrifices. The money changers allowed people to exchange their money into the proper currency for the temple offering (much like the currency-exchange booths at the international terminal in an airport). Those selling doves were providing animals for pilgrims to purchase for use as a sacrifice—animals they would not have been able to bring with them if they came from a long distance.

Forget business as usual, though; Jesus knows that a change is coming. In a few days he will offer himself as the complete and perfect sacrifice. The sacrificial system, which has become burdensome and oppressive, will no longer be needed, for Jesus is about to make atonement once and for all. For the whole world.

Think of this story as an enacted parable. This is Jesus telling the merchants that their services will no longer be needed. The perfect Lamb of God is about to be offered up for the life of the world.

I have heard other preachers say that there is absolutely nothing you can do to make God love you anymore than God loves you right now. No offering, no sacrifice, no heroic spiritual act can persuade God to look upon you with favor, because God already does. The Lord has already provided everything that is needed for us to be made right.

The only sacrifice required is to offer ourselves.

Lord Jesus, you are the spotless Lamb. I praise you that you have already made atonement for my sin. You have offered yourself up in my place. Help me today to receive that gift and to give myself as the proper offering. In your name, Amen.

Mark 11:20-26

The thing about this passage that immediately grabs our attention is that the fig tree Jesus cursed a few verses earlier has now withered. What Jesus spoke has come to pass. Even more to the point, Jesus confers upon his disciples the same kind of power. "Whatever you ask for in prayer, believe that you have received it, and it will be yours."

Does Jesus literally mean that we can curse fig trees and move mountains if we only believe enough? This question captivates our imaginations. It also stirs up all kinds of unhealthy assumptions. If you pray for something and it doesn't happen, does that mean you didn't believe strongly enough?

But all of this misses what I think is the true key to the passage. It's tucked away at the end: "And when you stand praying, if you hold anything against anyone, forgive him, so that your Father in heaven may forgive your sins."

There is a lot about prayer that I can neither understand nor explain. I cannot explain why some genuine prayers do not appear to come receive answers. Some of the most faithful people I have known have prayed for things they didn't get.

But one thing is as clear as the blue sky above my head this morning. Nothing blocks the flow of spiritual power in our lives like an unforgiving spirit. If we harbor resentments or hold on to grudges or let anger or frustration towards someone fester in our hearts and minds, it will absolutely limit the power of our prayers. We can read all the books we want on how to have a better prayer life, but if we don't tend to the unforgiveness within us, we will become increasingly powerless in the spiritual realm because we will be allowing the enemy to continue exerting its power.

I live across the street from Tinker Mountain. I rather doubt that if I squint my eyes hard enough and pray fervently enough, I can make that mountain disappear. I don't think this is what Jesus has in mind in the passage. But I know beyond a shadow of a doubt that if I examine closely enough the parts of my life where I am struggling or feeling limited, I will likely find a need to express or experience forgiveness.

And that is a prayer God will always be glad to answer.

Father, forgive my unwillingness to forgive. And convict me of my need to do so. Through Christ, Amen.

Mark 11:27-33

Jesus was asked lots of questions. Some of them he was glad to answer. "Will you heal my son?" "Will you teach us to pray?" "How will we feed this many people?" These are questions that seek a genuine answer built on a genuine trust in the power of the Son of God, and Jesus was glad to answer them.

But there are other questions that Jesus avoided or ignored because he knew that they were not asked out of a genuine search for truth. Such questions were either based on the wrong premise, such as, "Will you give us the seats of honor in your kingdom?" or based on an effort to avoid the truth and trap Jesus with his words, such as, "What is the greatest commandment?"

It is no small thing to learn to ask the right questions.

In today's reading, the authorities question Jesus. They want to know by what authority he does all "these things," a reference to the miracles and teachings for which he is responsible. But why do they ask? It's not because they have a genuine desire to better understand the nature of true authority. Quite the opposite is true. You can tell from the tone of the conversation that they already think they know what the answer is supposed to be, and their question is just a way of confirming what they already think they know.

Jesus will have none of it. He won't be drawn into their manipulative ways. For those who really want to know truth, Jesus will be glad to reveal himself. That is, after all, why he came into the world in the first place. He is truth in the flesh, and he does not begrudge genuine seekers who truly want to know. But for those who only want to reinforce their preconceived notions or who are looking for an excuse to avoid truth, Jesus won't bother.

It is fine for us to ask questions. In fact, we can ask anything we want. God is big enough to handle it. But are we willing to receive truth, even if it moves us in unexpected directions?

Lord Jesus, I want to know truth, and yet at the same time I want to avoid it. I often find ways of reinforcing my preferred views of the world rather than surrendering myself to the real truth you want to reveal to me. Help me today to be a genuine seeker. Help me to ask good questions and not to be afraid of the answers you will give. Through Christ, Amen.

Mark 12:35-40

Have you noticed how often Jesus quotes Scripture? From his forty-day period of testing and fasting in the wilderness, right on up through his final moments on the cross, Jesus frequently cited verses from his Bible (what we now call the Old Testament).

He did so as a way of interpreting present events in light of God's prior revelation. It was Jesus' way of showing that what happened in the present moment was part of God's plan, even though the present events rarely fit the expectations most people around him had formed in their minds. Most folks had already determined what it would look like when God finally got God's way. Whatever people were expecting, it certainly did not look like a homeless, itinerant rabbi who got himself executed.

Nowhere is that tension more evident than in today's reading. Jesus quotes Psalm 110:1, a psalm of King David. David originally wrote those words to celebrate God's upholding and blessing of the office of king. The kingship was understood to be a sign of God's ruling presence with the people.

But Jesus reinterprets the verse to show that, in fact, the Scriptures had always been pointing to him. This is critical to understand. The purpose of Scripture, from beginning to end, is to reveal Christ. Even in the Old Testament, hundreds and thousands of years before Jesus' coming as an incarnate human being, the Bible was preparing the way for the coming of Christ.

The Bible is not primarily a rulebook, though it certainly has important rules in it. The Bible is not primarily a practical guide for successful living, though it certainly has important principles that we should follow. The Bible is not primarily an index of solutions to all our problems, though we would certainly find that many of our problems would diminish if we obeyed what it said. The Bible is first and foremost the story of how God has acted on our behalf to save us through the person and the work of Jesus Christ. The Bible is the grand narrative of how God has done for us what we could not do for ourselves.

"The Lord says to my Lord: 'Sit at my right hand until I put your enemies under your feet'" (Ps 110:1). That is a story that is worth being a part of!

Lord God, from the moment we first fell into sin, you have been preparing the way to save us. Thank you for Jesus, who is that way. Help me today to see the story of my life in the light of your story, told through Jesus. Amen.

Mark 12:41-44

"Jesus sat down opposite the place where the offerings were put and watched the crowd."

As a pastor, I have always chosen not to know who contributes what to our church. For one thing, it minimizes the likelihood that someone will accuse me of showing favoritism to the big donors, because I don't know who those big donors are.

For another thing, it simply avoids the awkwardness of being involved in such a personal matter in people's lives. Have you noticed how in today's culture we discuss the most private sexual habits of people without blushing, but we would die before we'd talk about how much money we make and what we do with it?

But Jesus clearly is not bothered by that awkwardness. In today's reading, he chooses a place to sit precisely because it will enable him to see directly who is giving what. The only reason we can now celebrate the widow's small and seemingly insignificant offering is because Jesus was watching.

Jesus pays attention to what we do with what we have because Jesus cares greatly about what we do with what we have. "His eye is on the sparrow, and I know he watches me," goes the old song. Yes, but is this a good thing or a bad thing?

God is not some cosmic cop looking down from heaven to monitor our every move so that he can zap us the moment we make a mistake. God gives us enormous freedom. And I think that in much the same way a parent rejoices as he watches a child grow into the freedom of young adulthood and begin to exercise it in a healthy and mature way, God also rejoices in our exercise of our freedom.

And God rejoices when we freely choose to use what we have in ways that bless the Lord and others. And God will know because God watches. And God watches out of love.

Lord God, before a thought is on my lips you already know it completely. Help me to conduct myself today in such a way as to bring joy and pleasure to you. Through Christ, Amen.

Mark 13:1-2

Scientists in Britain recently made a fascinating discovery. After centuries of mystery and debate, they finally located the body of King Richard III, who was killed in battle in 1485. The location of his grave was lost to history until February 2013, when DNA tests confirmed that they had indeed found the late king's final resting place.

Here's what I find interesting. King Richard was buried underneath a parking lot! What irony. A man who was once a king, commanding armies and leading an empire, now had a minivan parked over his head so a mom could take her eight-year-old to soccer practice!

The things that seem so certain and powerful in their time will eventually come to nothing. We humans are not permanent fixtures around here, and neither are the things we build—not even our armies and the empires they protect. Only God is eternal.

Outside the temple in Jerusalem, the disciples were awed by the impressive structure. (This may have been the first time in their lives that they had been to the Holy City.) Jesus said, "Do you see all these great buildings? Not one stone here will be left on another."

Not even our religious institutions can guarantee the permanence we want. Jesus says this not to scare us but to point us to the truth. Only God is eternal. And only those who ground their lives in God will share in that gift.

Holy God, I confess that I try to ground my life in things that seem permanent. Today much of my energy will be spent trying to guarantee my existence. But help me to find my true life in you and in you alone. Help me to give myself to the tasks and the people that you put before me today, but help me to do so with an eye towards your eternity. Through Christ, the Eternal One, Amen.

Mark 13:3-31

As I write these words, it is the seventieth anniversary of D-Day. Seventy years ago today, Allied forces stormed the beaches of Normandy in a push to drive the Nazis out of occupied France. It was the largest military invasion force in history. Those who participated in that event could tell you firsthand the kind of furor and horror that is unleashed when man turns his weapons against man.

Let's be clear: no nation is without fault. No empire is perfectly righteous. Even still, there is good and there is evil, and when they do battle here in the temporal realm, there is often hell to pay. Just ask the veterans of D-Day or Iwo Jima or Afghanistan or any of the other countless battles that have been waged in the history of man's fight with man.

In Mark 13, Jesus uses alarming language to describe the crisis that awaits when the day of judgment comes. Christians often disagree over how to best interpret passages such as these. Premillennialists, for example, see this as part of a literal script detailing an exact sequence of events that will be a prelude to Christ's second coming. Others read this text more symbolically, believing that apocalyptic language has its own logic that can't be squeezed too easily into a neat grid predicting the future.

But however one chooses to interpret the specifics of a passage like this, one thing is inescapable. Far beyond the immediate temporal realm, an ultimate battle between God and evil is being waged, and when the final invasion occurs, some will find that there is hell to pay.

We don't care much for images of judgment like the ones this story holds out for us. We'd rather focus on Jesus as the nice guy who wants everybody to get along with each other. But Jesus is the embodiment—the incarnation—of truth. And the thing about truth is that it calls out and exposes what is not true. There can be no "good news" without judgment, because the good news is that evil will be destroyed.

Historians tell us that the outcome of WWII was basically determined on D-Day—at least in Europe. Once the Allies established that beachhead, it was more or less a given that the Nazis would be defeated. Even still, the war raged on for many more months, with many more casualties.

The same is true with us. The battle rages on, but the outcome has already been determined. When Jesus rose from the dead, he assured us of God's final triumph. If our trust is in Christ, we can read passages like Mark 13 without fear.

Holy God, I rejoice that you will have the last word, and that it will be good. Amen.

Mark 14:1-11

The kingdom of God is apparently wracked with wastefulness and inefficiency. Just think of some of the stories Jesus told. A shepherd with a hundred sheep leaves behind the ninety-nine good ones and goes off in search of the one knucklehead who managed to get lost. A father with two sons watches a third of his wealth get blown on booze and women and then throws a lavish party when the offending son crawls back home. A man sells everything he has so he can buy a field—not because he cares about the field itself but because of single piece of buried treasure that lies within it.

And now this. A woman takes a jar of extremely expensive perfume and pours it on Jesus' head. She doesn't simply uncork the thing and dab some of it on Jesus. She breaks the jar, making it impossible ever to use it for anything else, and then pours the whole thing out, right down to the last drop. Others in the room look on with horror. How ridiculously wasteful! "Think of how much more wisely this could have been used," the chair of the endowment committee protests.

Even if we ignore the fact that their alleged concern for the poor is disingenuous, we have to agree with their assessment. This woman has acted wastefully. Someone please sign her up for financial literacy 101!

But Jesus praises her for the act, for she recognizes what no one else seems capable of seeing. Jesus is about to go to the cross in the most lavish act of grace anyone could imagine. His body will be broken and his blood poured out. It will be wasteful by any standard—undeserved, unmerited, unmeasured. "Surely there is a more efficient way to do this," we think.

And all the while, that perfume is dripping through the cracks in the floorboards of Simon's house, its pungently sweet smell reminding us that a different kind of calculus is at work here. This woman's bizarre behavior is what we might call a "sign-act." She is proclaiming the truth about our lavishly wasteful Lord, even though in this case she never utters a word.

May God make us just foolish enough to live out of lavish and wasteful grace.

Holy God, I confess that I am so measured and reserved in the giving of myself, while you have poured yourself out fully on the cross. Help me to view my life and my relationships in the light of your lavish grace. Through Christ, Amen.

Mark 14:12-26

". . . . when it was customary to sacrifice the Passover lamb."

Believers will quickly recognize this as the story of the Last Supper, a story of supreme significance to us because it is the birth of Communion—the sacred meal instituted by Jesus as a way for his followers to remember and give thanks for his sacrificial death and triumphant resurrection.

But there is a temptation to overlook a simple detail of this story. The Last Supper occurred as part of the regular observance of Jewish religious practice, "when it was customary to sacrifice the Passover lambs." Jesus was a faithful, observant Jew. His life was shaped by the routine practices of his Jewish faith, even as he faced the coming crisis of his arrest and crucifixion. Yes, Jesus reinterpreted those traditional practices and gave them new meaning in light of the new covenant he created, but that New Covenant didn't simply materialize out of thin air. Jesus' life and ministry was in continuity with the practices of the faith handed down to him.

In our modern era, there is a fascination with newness and novelty. The new smartphone is automatically assumed to be better than the old smartphone, even though the old one still has features I haven't fully figured out how to use.

Added to this is the strong emphasis within evangelicalism on personal religious experience. It's not enough to know or believe certain things; one must also feel certain things. (And the emotional experience is usually given more weight than the cognitive one.)

The end result is a general disdain for routine and regular practice. That is just "going through the motions," we are told. How many times have I heard the old adage, "A read prayer is a dead prayer," as though I could never possibly learn anything from the devotional lives of others? What really matters is experiencing God, which we are told can happen anywhere and anytime. There is no need for ritual.

There is a degree of truth in this. God's transcendent glory can become immanently present in the most unexpected ways and places. And it is of first importance to know personally that one has been saved. To use an old analogy, showing up for church doesn't make one a Christian any more than sleeping in a garage makes one a Buick! Going through motions, by itself, is not enough.

But routine and regular practice still matter. Emotional experience alone cannot sustain us over time. We need a disciplined pattern of spiritual practice that can provide the structure on which to build our spiritual lives. If Jesus found it necessary to structure his life around the basic practices of his faith, such as showing up at the synagogue on the Sabbath, then we would be fools of the highest order to assume that we can live without such practices.

Listening to Christian radio while driving around running errands can help to momentarily lift our thoughts toward God. This is a good thing. But it is a poor substitute for regular, disciplined scriptural meditation and prayer. Staying home on a Sunday morning and watching Joel Osteen can give us vaguely warm religious sentiments (and all from the comfort of our living rooms), but it is not going to require us to learn what it means to live and worship in community with all those quirky people down at the church. Dropping a few dollars in the Salvation Army kettle outside Walmart at Christmas can help us feel good for a moment, but it is not going to discipline our overall financial lives the way that tithing will.

We need to be engaged in routine, regular practice. Our lives need to be disciplined by the structures of our faith. If it was good enough for Jesus, it should be good enough for us as well!

Lord Jesus, thank you that you saw fit to settle into the routines of your people. Help me today to see the routines of my life infused with holiness and meaning. Amen.

Mark 14:27-31

One of the reasons Scripture is so powerful is its brutal honesty when it comes to naming our human condition. There are no efforts to dress things up or to make our situation look like anything other than what it is. "As for man, his days are like grass, he flourishes like a flower of the field; the wind blows over it and it is gone," says Psalm 103:15-16. These are harsh words in a culture that is obsessed with finding the fountain of youth.

And now this. Jesus says to Peter, "You will all fall away." Jesus says as plain as day that Peter and all the disciples will fail miserably when the moment of testing comes. Which is exactly what happens.

We want to believe in our own basic goodness. Sure, we make a few mistakes along the way, but on the whole we are honest, hard-working, truthful, upright, loyal, faithful, decent people who want to do the right thing. We just need a little help getting over the top. So God was on to something when God acted to save us. Right?

But Scripture says otherwise. We are sinners. We are selfish and fearful and disloyal and lustful and greedy, and we are generally more interested in saving our own skin than we are in pursuing the kingdom of God.

Jesus knew this. He wasn't confused or fooled by anything. And yet he welcomed Peter to the table for the last supper anyway. Knowing full well what was coming, Jesus shared the bread and the cup with the very ones who would betray and desert him.

If that offends us, then maybe we are ready for the first time to understand the true meaning of grace. Grace is not about God giving us a little extra dose of goodness and righteousness to top off our tank. It is about God completely exchanging God's righteousness for our unrighteousness.

"But God demonstrates his own love for us in this," writes Paul in Romans 5:8, "that while we were still sinners, Christ died for us." Therein lies our only hope.

Gracious God, I want so badly to believe that I am good person. Help me to lay aside the shallow excuses and the rationalizations that fill my life each day. Help me to recognize that true goodness only begins when I acknowledge my need for you. Through Christ, Amen.

Mark 14:32-42

"[Jesus] began to be greatly distressed and troubled."

Yesterday at a funeral for one of the long-time saints of our church, we were reminded that the Bible, especially the book of Psalms, is full of expressions of grief, lament, and anger. These passages not only help us express what we are feeling but also help us bring those feelings before God. The good news is that we don't have to get all "prettied up" and bring everything to a positive resolution before we can come to God. We can just be honest about our experience, even when that experience leaves us in a not-so-happy place.

Jesus certainly wasn't afraid of that kind of honesty. On the night before his crucifixion, he cried out in anguish, "Let this cup pass from me." He did not want to face what was before him, and he admitted it. We are even told that his anguish was so great that his sweat become like drops of blood.

We need to be willing to be greatly distressed and troubled— about ourselves and about our world. There is much about this life that is not what it should be. International affairs and private experiences remind us that there is pain and sorrow, and we need the courage of our faith to be honest about this.

Jesus was able to do so because he trusted the Father's goodness. He could cry out in anguish because he knew that his Father's love would eventually overwhelm even his suffering. "Never the less, not my will but yours." This is the prayer of someone who can face the darkness with the assurance of Divine love.

Holy Father, help me to be honest about my struggles today.
Prevent me from the laziness of mind that refuses to acknowledge

pain and hardship for what it is. And yet also give me the courage of my convictions to know that you are God and that you are good, and that in your time all things shall be well. Amen.

Mark 14:43-52

Why did Judas do it? What prompted him to betray Jesus for a few silver coins? People have pondered this question for centuries, speculating as to his motives. Some have said that Judas was hoping to prompt Jesus to act. By bringing a detachment of Roman soldiers, he could force Jesus to finally start the great uprising against Rome that everybody wanted. Others have suggested that Judas was just greedy and wanted a few silver coins.

The fact is that we do not know why Judas did it, because the Scriptures never tell. The Bible generally isn't interested in the kind of probing interiority we see in the modern psychodrama. The Bible simply tells us that Judas betrayed Jesus because, well, Judas was a betrayer. Whatever other motives we may want to assign to him, that's what betrayers do. Betrayers betray.

This is where the power of Scripture lies. If we could assign a precise explanation to Judas's behavior, then we could distance ourselves from it. If we could attribute his actions to this or to that, then we could convince ourselves that, for all the bad things we may do, we would never do this or that. Sure, I may fudge on my income tax returns a little bit (just to keep what is rightfully mine), but I would never knowingly defraud someone. Right?

Of all the lies we tell, the worst are the ones we tell ourselves.

Meanwhile, the truth is that betrayers betray, liars lie, cheaters cheat, lusters lust, deceivers deceive, and thieves steal. Our motives for such things are secondary at best. They are simply what those people (and sometimes we) do. "By their fruit you shall know them," Jesus says in Matthew 7.

But the good news is that Jesus goes forward to the cross, just as the Father's plan required. "But the Scriptures must be fulfilled,"

Jesus said as Judas approached him with that band of armed guards. This was all part of God's plan to save us.

From ourselves.

Father, I confess to my mixed and confused motives. Even when I want to do good, I find that bad is right there with me. Left to my own resources, there is no pure good in me. But thank you that you have loved me through Christ in spite of myself. Help me to love others in the same way you have loved me. Amen.

Mark 14:53-65

Fans of the hit series *24* were excited to see Jack Bauer back in action during the 2014 television season. After four years in hiding, the former federal agent was once again trying to save the world from evil and terror. In almost every episode of this show, there is a life-or-death moment when it appears that the end has come, either for Jack or for those in his charge. But just when things look the bleakest, Jack finds a way to save the day—usually at the expense of someone else who is no match for his skill and physical prowess.

We like stories that go this way. We want to see the "good guys" win. And if that happens to include a little butt-kickin' for the bad guys, then so much the better. He with the most guns wins, right?

But here is Jesus standing before his accusers, and he barely opens his mouth. He won't even try to defend himself against the false charges leveled at him. And there will be no effort to try to mentally outsmart or physically overcome his captors so that he can escape. He willingly submits himself to what is about to happen.

That's because Jesus is operating by a different narrative. Jesus chooses the way of suffering love. He has no need to try to "win" in the moment or to direct events toward the outcome he desires. He will not try to vindicate himself because he trusts the Father's plan to accomplish his purposes, even when that plan necessarily involves suffering in the moment.

Those who choose to follow Jesus are called to choose that same way. We can let go of the need to "win" in every situation and the desire to constantly vindicate ourselves because we too can trust that the Father's plan is far better than anything we could conceive, even when that plan is going to cost us dearly.

It is unlikely that any of us will be called on today to save the world from evil or terror. But is very likely that at some point we will be called to love someone when it is inconvenient or costly. Can we show that love, even when it is unlikely that doing so will produce the results we desire? How would our marriages and families be different if we loved that way? What would the fellowship of our churches look like? How would our relationships with our neighbors be transformed? What would be the tone of our public discourse, especially with those with whom we disagree?

Are we truly ready to love the way Jesus loves?

Father, may that question be foremost in my mind in every interaction I have this day. Amen.

Mark 14:66-72

What do you do when you blow it?

We often plow through life unaware of the damage we are doing. One of the characteristics of our self-centered and morally relativistic culture is that it conceals the reality of our brokenness. Our world doesn't give us many resources by which to even recognize the presence of sin in our lives.

But every now and then, it slaps us in the face. Every now and then, we are forced to confront the reality that we have failed miserably—failed to live by the standards that we thought were guiding our own behavior. What do we do when that happens? Where do we turn?

It happened to Peter. He heard the cock crow, and suddenly it hit him: he had denied his Lord. Three times, just like Jesus had said he would! Peter had refused to believe it at first. "No, Lord," Peter had said, "I will never disown you." But there in the smoky air of those pre-dawn hours, Peter had no choice but to admit it. He had blown it. And he broke down and wept.

We need to pray for the grace to weep over our sin. We are so quick to rationalize our behavior. We can give lots of excuses, or we can simply ignore the situation altogether. But until we can see ourselves as we really are, we won't acknowledge our need for salvation. A life preserver means nothing to people who don't realize they are drowning.

Peter broke down and wept. It had to be the darkest hour of his life. But Peter's story did not end there, because neither did Jesus' story. Three days later, Jesus was alive again. And to whom did he come back?

To the one who had wept over his sin against Jesus.

Lord Jesus, make me painfully aware today of my failings so that I can be joyfully aware of your grace. Amen.

Mark 15:1-15

There is a curious line tucked into the middle of today's reading that I've never really noticed until now. Pilate is trying to navigate his way through the politically difficult situation of Jesus' so-called trial. He is not concerned with doing the right thing; he just wants to do whatever is going to maintain the status quo and prevent an uprising. If things get out of control in Jerusalem, it's not going to be good for his career as a Roman governor.

Seeing a possible way out, he remembers that he has a custom of releasing one prisoner each year during the Feast of the Passover. Think of it as a good-will gesture on the part of the occupying forces. And that's where Mark's Gospel inserts this little observation: Pilate knew that the chief priests had handed Jesus over to him out of envy. Maybe he can persuade the crowd to call for Jesus' release because this is all about envy in the first place.

Pilate may have lacked a few things in the virtue department. Again, he was more concerned with doing what was expedient than with doing what was right. But Pilate was no dummy, either. He understood a thing or two about the human condition. For all the high-minded religious language the chief priests were using, Pilate knew that this was really about envy. The priests were envious of Jesus.

We know that from the Divine perspective, Jesus was crucified to make atonement for our sins. The Father sent the Son to die on a cross so that we could be reconciled to God and to each other. This was the Father's plan from the beginning. But when we look at the story from the human perspective, what factors motivated the human actors in this drama to do the things they did? Could it be that the Son of God was nailed to a cross for something as base and mundane as envy?

I have two daughters. In many ways, they are the best of friends. One of my great joys is listening to them giggle while they play together. But it is amazing how quickly their emotions can turn from laughter to tears the moment one of them becomes jealous of the other. If one of them gets something that the other thinks she should have, the sisters can instantly go from being the best of friends to being mortal enemies. This is the power of envy.

The Bible repeatedly warns us to guard against envy. The opening lines of James 4 tell us that wanting what others have leads to covetousness and even murder. In the Sermon on the Mount, Jesus warns against the spiritual dangers of contempt towards others. It doesn't take a great stretch of the imagination to see how envy plays into that. Simply put, envy is toxic to the spirit.

It's an odd thing to say, but maybe today we should take a word of advice from Pilate. Let's be on guard against the power of envy at work in our lives.

Heavenly Father, you make your sun shine on the evil and the good, and you give to everyone as you see fit. Help me today to rejoice in the ways you provide for me, and save me from keeping score of how you do the same for others. Teach me to be content with your grace, which alone is sufficient for my needs. Through Christ, Amen.

Mark 15:16-20

One wonders what prompted the soldiers in this passage to act like they did. Why are they so mean and hateful towards Jesus? This is their first interaction with him. They've had no stake so far in the controversies surrounding him, no reason to hate him. What's their motivation? Obviously, we cannot know for sure. These characters make a brief cameo appearance in this scene and then promptly exit the stage without telling us what's going on inside their minds. But we can speculate.

I imagine that being a Roman soldier is a hard life. It's a meager existence, economically speaking. You aren't paid much, you are stationed far from home, you are surrounded by hard circumstances in a world defined by violence, and somewhere in the back of your mind you know that you are just a cog in a giant machine called Empire. The end result is that you become a cynic. You are hard-boiled, edgy, crusty. You trust no one, you don't expect anyone to have your best interests in mind, and you certainly don't look for things like truth and beauty. You just want to survive.

Then along comes some poor chap named Jesus who has been accused of something or other against the Empire. You don't care about the details. They don't matter. You see this sort of thing all the time. It's just another day on the job. You might as well have a little fun and relieve your boredom.

"Hey, let's stick a crown of thorns on this one's head," says someone. That ought to get a laugh.

I know I am speculating, but I don't think I am too far afield. It doesn't take a well-developed imagination to recognize the negative power of cynicism. Cynicism is a defense mechanism. It protects us from the need to make ourselves vulnerable in a world that would be all too happy to take advantage of us.

But that protection comes at a great cost, for it closes us off to the possibility of encountering real truth and real beauty when we see it. I've heard it said that a cynical mind is a lazy mind, for it refuses to spend the effort and energy needed to process the world in an authentic way. Cynicism immediately writes everything off as being not worth the trouble.

I write these words partly as confession. I know myself well enough to know that I have a tendency towards cynicism. It is easy for me to drop into that hard-edged, crusty attitude and close myself off. And I imagine the same is true for most everybody reading this. It's easier to take the path of least resistance than it is to stay open to the possibilities of love and life and transformation.

The Son of God—Truth and Beauty Incarnate—was standing right before the soldiers, and they couldn't see it. Let's not make the same mistake.

Lord Jesus, keep my mind and my spirit open and receptive today. Give me the grace to refuse the temptation to become cynical and closed. Reveal your truth to me. In your name I pray, Amen.

Mark 15:21-32

"Simon . . . was passing by . . . and they forced him to carry the cross."

It has always struck me as odd that Mark included this detail in his account of the crucifixion. Jesus is obviously the center of the action. He is going to the cross to reconcile the world to the Father. For the reader of the Scriptures, all eyes are on him. But then here comes Simon the Cyrene, who just happens to be passing through. He's had no part in the unfolding drama, and yet he gets pressed into service, forced by the Roman officials to carry Jesus' cross for part of the journey up Golgotha.

Is this not the pattern of true discipleship? There we are, just going about our routine lives, minding our own business, doing the things that our daily responsibilities require from us, when all of a sudden we find ourselves being asked to carry the cross for a little while. We weren't looking for it or asking for it, but there it is all the same. When those moments come, will we march up Golgotha with Jesus?

Your boss announces a new initiative that you know is morally questionable. What are you going to do? You wake up one day and discover that your spouse has had an affair. What are you going to do? Your neighbor has a crisis, and you are the only one who seems to be able to provide counsel and comfort. What are you going to do? Your grown child moves out into a way of life that seems to reject everything you've modeled. What are you going to do? How are you going to represent Christ in that moment?

Somewhere, somehow, we are each going to be asked to carry Jesus' cross. That cross is not a distraction or a detour on the journey of discipleship. It is the journey.

Lord Jesus, help me remember and embody your words when you said that anyone who would come after you must take up his cross. Amen.

Mark 15:33-38

If I were to sing part of the lines to a popular song, chances are good your mind would automatically fill in the next line or phrase. Good or bad, popular music occupies a space in our collective memory, and when that collective memory is tapped, things flow out of it quite naturally. It may seem like an inappropriate analogy given the grim circumstances, but I think a similar thing is going on in the crucifixion.

"My God, my God, why have you forsaken me?"

Those words sound haunting coming from the lips of Jesus. Is the Son really accusing the Father of abandoning him? Well, yes and no. Jesus is actually quoting Scripture—Psalm 22:1, to be exact. David wrote this particular psalm. We don't know the precise circumstances in which David wrote these words, but he was clearly going through a challenging and difficult time. In the moment God felt far away, and David was honest enough to say so. This is part of the function of the psalms; they provide a place to put our emotions and our experiences. Both the good and the bad of life can be offered up as a kind of prayer to God.

This is what Jesus does on the cross. In his moment of pain, Jesus reaches back into the treasure trove of Scripture to express what he is experiencing. He uses the Scriptures to be honest with God. This is the heart of prayer. Whatever we are going through, there is probably something in Scripture that can resonate with the experience.

But there is more going on here. For the ancient Jews the Scriptures, especially the psalms, functioned much like popular music does for our culture. Scripture occupied a central place in their collective conscience. Just recite a line or two of Scripture, and others will find that their minds automatically fill in the rest of the passage. Quote the first line of a psalm, and the entire psalm comes to mind.

That makes Psalm 22 an interesting choice for Jesus to quote. While the psalm begins by expressing dismay over feelings of rejection, it changes tone in verse 19. David begins to affirm that God will deliver him from his enemies, even though the present circumstances would seem to suggest otherwise. And the psalm ends with David affirming God's goodness and triumph. (I suggest you stop for a moment to read the entire psalm for yourself and see what I mean.)

Jesus cries out in agony from the cross. He is honest about the pain and the feelings of rejection. But he does so using a psalm that ultimately affirms God's triumph—a triumph that will be seen three days later. Even in his death, Jesus is pointing us to the goodness of God.

Eloi, eloi, lama sabachthani? Indeed.

Gracious God, you see and know all things, so there is no use in me trying to hide the reality of my experiences from you. Help me to trust you enough today to be honest about what I am thinking and feeling. But help me also to trust in your triumph over the sorrows and heartaches I will encounter today. Through Christ, Amen.

Mark 15:42-47

"Mary Magdalene and Mary the mother of Joses saw where he was laid."

This rather straightforward sentence in Mark's account of the story is of first importance. These women saw it with their own eyes: Jesus' body was laid in a tomb and sealed with a large rock. There could be no doubt that Jesus was dead. Whatever hope they might have had that somehow the situation could be redeemed—that maybe somehow, some way, it didn't have to end like this—such hopes disappeared when they saw Jesus buried in a sealed tomb.

This is where the gospel meets real life. We are prone to think of religion as a set of "higher principles" or abstract values to ponder and pursue. Some might say that spirituality is what's happening when we are thinking our best thoughts and are striving to be our best selves. But here is religion that meets us squarely in the midst of the darkest and most vile moments of life. Here is a God who comes down into the dusty, poverty-stricken world of unsophisticated peasants and dies. Here is a spirituality that embraces death and all that goes with it.

As readers of the story, we know what happens next. In the very next verse, those same women go back to the same tomb three days later and witness something incredible. But we need to slow down our rush to Sunday morning. We need to stop for a moment at the tomb on Friday. We need to let the image of Jesus' burial sink into our hearts and minds for a moment.

Because if we don't, then this story won't have much to offer us. Yes, we believe in the resurrection. As believers, we stake our lives on that hope. But while we wait for that hope to be realized, we continue to live in a world of death and decay. Resurrection doesn't happen away from or apart from the very real (and sometimes very hard) lives that we lead in the real world. That's why we need a spirituality that is big enough to embrace the reality that our senses are reporting to us every day. There may be religions that begin with us sitting under a tree and getting alone with our thoughts, but the gospel begins with us standing beside a recently opened tomb where a loved one has just been laid.

Our God is big enough to secure our lives because God is also big enough to embrace our deaths, and all that goes with them.

Gracious God, thank you for the witness of these women who refused to avert their gaze when Jesus was laid in a tomb. Help me to see all that happens today—the good and even the bad—as part of my journey with the risen Lord. Through Christ, Amen.

Mark 16:1-8

When my oldest daughter was first learning to write stories in school she was taught that every good story has a beginning, a middle, and an end. In other words, there is an identifiable progression of the plot that starts somewhere, goes somewhere, and then ends with an understandable resolution of the conflict that was driving the story. You cannot leave people hanging.

When Mark penned his Gospel, he seems to have not been aware of this important narrative technique. The earliest versions of Mark that are available to us end at verse 8. The final passage in our modern translations (vv. 9-20) seems to have been added later. Perhaps there was originally a different ending that has since been lost to us, but the oldest known manuscript of Mark leaves off with the women running away from the tomb in fear. That's strange. What will become of them? And what about the news they carry? How will this bizarre story of an empty tomb be resolved?

My daughter's teacher might disagree, but I think this is a powerful way to end the story. The open-ended narrative invites us to consider how we will provide the answers to these questions with our lives. The tomb is empty. So what? What difference is that going to make? What are we going to do with that bit of news? How will our lives be different when we walk away from the open grave?

Don't get me wrong. The objective truth of the resurrection is not in doubt for Mark or for any of the other Gospel writers. Our individual experience is not the measure for whether Jesus really was raised from the dead. But to a certain extent, the impact of the resurrection does remain to be seen. We can walk away from Easter and try to carry on with our lives as though nothing has really changed.

Or we, like the women, can come to recognize that because of what happened that morning, nothing will ever be the same again.

That first Easter has now come and gone, but you and I are still in the middle of the story. How will it end for us?

Heavenly Father, the mystery of the resurrection still seems too good to be true, and yet all those who have gone before me in the faith lived as though everything else was dependent on it. Help me today to live in that same way, seeing all of life through the lens of the empty tomb. Through Christ, Amen.

Mark 16:9-20

There is an interesting tension hidden in this final story in Mark's Gospel. Jesus rebukes the disciples for their failure to believe the reports of Jesus' resurrection. And then he immediately commissions them to go out into the world and preach the gospel!

You can't help wondering why Jesus didn't come up with a better plan. We've been plodding along with this saga for sixteen chapters now. If, after all that has happened, these guys still struggle with doubt, then what business do they have representing Jesus?

The answer has at least something to do with the fact that there is no Plan B. Jesus called these people —for all their faults and foibles— to be his followers, his disciples. At this point he has staked the entire future of his Father's kingdom on them.

This is the nature of salvation. Jesus doesn't save humanity by acting outside of our humanity. He redeems our human condition entirely from within our human condition. Fear, doubt, weakness, struggle—these are not things that have to be demolished in order for the gospel to advance; by the power of God they become the very means by which that advance happens.

Later in the New Testament, the Apostle Paul will say, "We have this treasure in jars of clay to show that this all-surpassing power is from God and not from us." A jar of clay was understood in those days to be a fragile (though necessary) thing. By grace, our weakness and imperfection are transformed to become a vehicle for God's power.

This doesn't mean that things like fear and doubt and weakness are to be celebrated and encouraged. Despite the claims of our skeptical world, doubt is not a badge of honor. It does mean that such things are not excuses to avoid the call of God on our lives. If God can use the likes of Peter and the other disciples—these who denied and abandoned him—God can use us. After all that Mark has said to us in his Gospel account, he would be happy to know that we walked away understanding nothing other than this.

Gracious God, I can think of dozens of reasons why I am not qualified to be your disciple, yet you have chosen me anyway. Thank you that you have responded to me on the basis of your mercy and grace rather than on my accomplishments and credentials. Help me to trust your goodness working through me even when I have none to offer for myself. Through Christ, Amen.

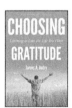

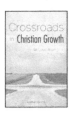

Crossroads in Christian Growth
W. Loyd Allen

Authentic Christian life presents spiritual crises and we struggle to find a hero walking with God at a crossroads. With wisdom and sincerity, W. Loyd Allen presents Jesus as our example and these crises as stages in the journey of growth we each take toward maturity in Christ.   *978-1-57312-753-0 164 pages/pb* **$15.00**

A Divine Duet
Ministry and Motherhood
Alicia Davis Porterfield, ed.

Each essay in this inspiring collection is as different as the mother-minister who wrote it, from theologians to chaplains, inner-city ministers to rural-poverty ministers, youth pastors to preachers, mothers who have adopted, birthed, and done both.   *978-1-57312-676-2 146 pages/pb* **$16.00**

The Exile and Beyond (All the Bible series)
Wayne Ballard

The Exile and Beyond brings to life the sacred literature of Israel and Judah that comprises the exilic and postexilic communities of faith. It covers Ezekiel, Isaiah, Haggai, Zechariah, Malachi, 1 & 2 Chronicles, Ezra, Nehemiah, Joel, Jonah, Song of Songs, Esther, and Daniel.   *978-1-57312-759-2 196 pages/pb* **$16.00**

Ezekiel (Smyth & Helwys Annual Bible Study series)
God's Presence in Performance
William D. Shiell

Through a four-session Bible study for individuals and groups, Shiell interprets the book of Ezekiel as a four-act drama to be told to those living out their faith in a strange, new place. Shiell encourages congregations to listen to God's call, accept where God has planted them, surrender the shame of their past, receive a new heart from God, and allow God to breathe new life into them.   *Teaching Guide 978-1-57312-755-4 192 pages/pb* **$14.00**

Study Guide 978-1-57312-756-1 126 pages/pb **$6.00**

Fierce Love
Desperate Measures for Desperate Times
Jeanie Miley

Fierce Love is about learning to see yourself and know yourself as a conduit of love, operating from a full heart instead of trying to find someone to whom you can hook up your emotional hose and fill up your empty heart.   *978-1-57312-810-0 276 pages/pb* **$18.00**

Five Hundred Miles
Reflections on Calling and Pilgrimage
Lauren Brewer Bass

Spain's Camino de Santiago, the Way of St. James, has been a cherished pilgrimage path for centuries, visited by countless people searching for healing, solace, purpose, and hope. These stories from her five-hundred-mile-walk is Lauren Brewer Bass's honest look at the often winding, always surprising journey of a calling.   *978-1-57312-812-4 142 pages/pb* **$16.00**

Galatians (Smyth & Helwys Bible Commentary)
Marion L. Soards and Darrell J. Pursiful

In Galatians, Paul endeavored to prevent the Gentile converts from embracing a version of the gospel that insisted on their observance of a form of the Mosaic Law. He saw with a unique clarity that such a message reduced the crucified Christ to being a mere agent of the Law. For Paul, the gospel of Jesus Christ alone, and him crucified, had no place in it for the claim that Law-observance was necessary for believers to experience the power of God's grace.   *978-1-57312-771-4 384 pages/hc* **$55.00**

God's Servants the Prophets
Bryan Bibb

God's Servants, the Prophets covers the Israelite and Judean prophetic literature from the preexilic period. It includes Amos, Hosea, Isaiah, Micah, Zephaniah, Nahum, Habakkuk, Jeremiah, and Obadiah.
978-1-57312-758-5 208 pages/pb **$16.00**

Hermeneutics of Hymnody
A Comprehensive and Integrated Approach to Understanding Hymns
Scotty Gray

Scotty Gray's *Hermeneutics of Hymnody* is a comprehensive and integrated approach to understanding hymns. It is unique in its holistic and interrelated exploration of seven of the broad facets of this most basic forms of Christian literature. A chapter is devoted to each and relates that facet to all of the others.   *978-157312-767-7 432 pages/pb* **$28.00**

If Jesus Isn't the Answer . . . He Sure Asks the Right Questions!
J. Daniel Day

Taking eleven of Jesus' questions as its core, Day invites readers into their own conversation with Jesus. Equal parts testimony, theological instruction, pastoral counseling, and autobiography, the book is ultimately an invitation to honest Christian discipleship.
978-1-57312-797-4 148 pages/pb **$16.00**

I'm Trying to Lead . . . Is Anybody Following?
The Challenge of Congregational Leadership in the
Postmodern World

Charles B. Bugg

Bugg provides us with a view of leadership that has theological
integrity, honors the diversity of church members, and reinforces
the brave hearts of church leaders who offer vision and take risks in the service of
Christ and the church.   *978-1-57312-731-8 136 pages/pb* **$13.00**

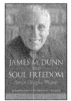

James M. Dunn and Soul Freedom
Aaron Douglas Weaver

James Milton Dunn, over the last fifty years, has been the most
aggressive Baptist proponent for religious liberty in the US. Soul
freedom—voluntary, uncoerced faith and an unfettered individual
conscience before God—is the basis of his understanding of church-
state separation and the historic Baptist basis of religious liberty.
                              978-1-57312-590-1 224 pages/pb **$18.00**

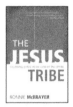

The Jesus Tribe
Following Christ in the Land of the Empire

Ronnie McBrayer

The Jesus Tribe fleshes out the implications, possibilities, contradic-
tions, and complexities of what it means to live within the Jesus
Tribe and in the shadow of the American Empire.
                              978-1-57312-592-5 208 pages/pb **$17.00**

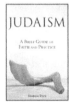

Judaism
A Brief Guide to Faith and Practice

Sharon Pace

Sharon Pace's newest book is a sensitive and comprehensive introduction to Judaism. How does belief in the One God and a universal
morality shape the way in which Jews see the world? How does one
find meaning in life and the courage to endure suffering? How does one mark joy
and forge community ties?   *978-1-57312-644-1 144 pages/pb* **$16.00**

Looking Around for God
The Strangely Reverent Observations of an Unconventional Christian

James A. Autry

Looking Around for God, Autry's tenth book, is in many ways his
most personal. In it he considers his unique life of faith and belief in
God. Autry is a former Fortune 500 executive, author, poet, and
consultant whose work has had a significant influence on leadership thinking.
                              978-157312-484-3 144 pages/pb **$16.00**

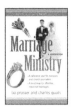

Marriage Ministry: A Guidebook
Bo Prosser and Charles Qualls

This book is equally helpful for ministers, for nearly/newlywed couples, and for thousands of couples across our land looking for fresh air in their marriages. *1-57312-432-X 160 pages/pb $16.00*

Meeting Jesus Today
For the Cautious, the Curious, and the Committed
Jeanie Miley

Meeting Jesus Today, ideal for both individual study and small groups, is intended to be used as a workbook. It is designed to move readers from studying the Scriptures and ideas within the chapters to recording their journey with the Living Christ.

978-1-57312-677-9 320 pages/pb $19.00

The Ministry Life
101 Tips for Ministers' Spouses
John and Anne Killinger

While no pastor does his or her work alone, roles for a spouse or partner are much more flexible and fluid now than they once were. Spouses who want to support their minister-mates' vocation may wonder where to begin. Whatever your talents may be, the Killingers have identified a way to put those gifts to work. *978-1-57312-769-1 252 pages/pb $19.00*

The Ministry Life
101 Tips for New Ministers
John Killinger

Sharing years of wisdom from more than fifty years in ministry and teaching, *The Ministry Life: 101 Tips for New Ministers* by John Killinger is filled with practical advice and wisdom for a minister's day-to-day tasks as well as advice on intellectual and spiritual habits to keep ministers of any age healthy and fulfilled. *978-1-57312-662-5 244 pages/pb $19.00*

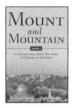

Mount and Mountain
Vol. 2: A Reverend and a Rabbi Talk About the Sermon on the Mount
Rami Shapiro and Michael Smith

This book, focused on the Sermon on the Mount, represents the second half of Mike and Rami's dialogue. In it, Mike and Rami explore the text of Jesus' sermon cooperatively, contributing perspectives drawn from their lives and religious traditions and seeking moments of illumination. *978-1-57312-654-0 254 pages/pb $19.00*

Of Mice and Ministers
Musings and Conversations About Life, Death, Grace, and Everything
Bert Montgomery

With stories about pains, joys, and everyday life, *Of Mice and Ministers* finds Jesus in some unlikely places and challenges us to do the same. From tattooed women ministers to saying the "N"-word to the brotherly kiss, Bert Montgomery takes seriously the lesson from Psalm 139—where can one go that God is not already there?   *978-1-57312-733-2 154 pages/pb* **$14.00**

Place Value
The Journey to Where You Are
Katie Sciba

Does a place have value? Can a place change us? Is it possible for God to use the place you are in to form you? From Victoria, Texas to Indonesia, Belize, Australia, and beyond, Katie Sciba's wanderlust serves as a framework to understand your own places of deep emotion and how God may have been weaving redemption around you all along.

978-157312-829-2 138 pages/pb **$15.00**

Preacher Breath
Sermon & Essays
Kyndall Rae Rothaus

"*Preacher Breath* is a worthy guide, leading the reader room by room with wisdom, depth, and a spiritual maturity far beyond her years, so that the preaching house becomes a holy, joyful home. . . . This book is soul kindle for a preacher's heart."   —Danielle Shroyer
Pastor, Author of *The Boundary-Breaking God*

978-1-57312-734-9 208 pages/pb **$16.00**

Quiet Faith
An Introvert's Guide to Spiritual Survival
Judson Edwards

In eight finely crafted chapters, Edwards looks at key issues like evangelism, interpreting the Bible, dealing with doubt, and surviving the church from the perspective of a confirmed, but sometimes reluctant, introvert. In the process, he offers some provocative insights that introverts will find helpful and reassuring.   *978-1-57312-681-6 144 pages/pb* **$15.00**

Reading Deuteronomy
(Reading the Old Testament series)
A Literary and Theological Commentary

Stephen L. Cook

A lost treasure for large segments of today's world, the book of Deuteronomy stirs deep longing for God and moves readers to a place of intimacy with divine otherness, holism, and will for person-centered community. The consistently theological interpretation reveals the centrality of this book for faith.
978-1-57312-757-8 286 pages/pb **$22.00**

Reflective Faith
A Theological Toolbox for Women

Susan M. Shaw

In *Reflective Faith*, Susan Shaw offers a set of tools to explore difficult issues of biblical interpretation, theology, church history, and ethics—especially as they relate to women. Reflective faith invites intellectual struggle and embraces the unknown; it is a way of discipleship, a way to love God with your mind, as well as your heart, your soul, and your strength.
978-1-57312-719-6 292 pages/pb **$24.00**
Workbook 978-1-57312-754-7 164 pages/pb **$12.00**

Sessions with Psalms (Sessions Bible Studies series)
Prayers for All Seasons

Eric and Alicia D. Porterfield

Useful to seminar leaders during preparation and group discussion, as well as in individual Bible study, *Sessions with Psalms* is a ten-session study designed to explore what it looks like for the words of the psalms to become the words of our prayers. Each session is followed by a thought-provoking page of questions.
978-1-57312-768-4 136 pages/pb **$14.00**

Sessions with Revelation
(Sessions Bible Studies series)
The Final Days of Evil

David Sapp

David Sapp's careful guide through Revelation demonstrates that it is a letter of hope for believers; it is less about the last days of history than it is about the last days of evil. Without eliminating its mystery, Sapp unlocks Revelation's central truths so that its relevance becomes clear.
978-1-57312-706-6 166 pages/pb **$14.00**

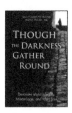

Though the Darkness Gather Round
Devotions about Infertility, Miscarriage, and Infant Loss
Mary Elizabeth Hill Hanchey and Erin McClain, eds.

Much courage is required to weather the long grief of infertility and the sudden grief of miscarriage and infant loss. This collection of devotions by men and women, ministers, chaplains, and lay leaders who can speak of such sorrow, is a much-needed resource and precious gift for families on this journey and the faith communities that walk beside them.

978-1-57312-811-7 180 pages/pb **$19.00**

Time for Supper
Invitations to Christ's Table
Brett Younger

Some scholars suggest that every meal in literature is a communion scene. Could every meal in the Bible be a communion text? Could every passage be an invitation to God's grace? These meditations on the Lord's Supper help us listen to the myriad of ways God invites us to gratefully, reverently, and joyfully share the cup of Christ. 978-1-57312-720-2 246 pages/pb **$18.00**

A Time to Laugh
Humor in the Bible
Mark E. Biddle

With characteristic liveliness, Mark E. Biddle explores the ways humor was intentionally incorporated into Scripture. Drawing on Biddle's command of Hebrew language and cultural subtleties, *A Time to Laugh* guides the reader through the stories of six biblical characters who did rather unexpected things. 978-1-57312-683-0 164 pages/pb **$14.00**

A True Hope
Jedi Perils and the Way of Jesus
Joshua Hays

Star Wars offers an accessible starting point for considering substantive issues of faith, philosophy, and ethics. In *A True Hope*, Joshua Hays explores some of these challenging ideas through the sayings of the Jedi Masters, examining the ways the worldview of the Jedi is at odds with that of the Bible. 978-1-57312-770-7 186 pages/pb **$18.00**

Word of God Across the Ages
Using Christian History in Preaching
Bill J. Leonard

In this third, enlarged edition, Bill J. Leonard returns to the roots of the Christian story to find in the lives of our faithful forebears examples of the potent presence of the gospel. Through these stories, those who preach today will be challenged and inspired as they pursue the divine Word in human history through the ages.   978-1-57312-828-5 174 pages/pb **$19.00**

The World Is Waiting for You
Celebrating the 50th Ordination Anniversary of Addie Davis
Pamela R. Durso & LeAnn Gunter Johns, eds.

Hope for the church and the world is alive and well in the words of these gifted women. Keen insight, delightful observations, profound courage, and a gift for communicating the good news are woven throughout these sermons. The Spirit so evident in Addie's calling clearly continues in her legacy.   978-1-57312-732-5 224 pages/pb **$18.00**

William J. Reynolds
Church Musician
David W. Music

William J. Reynolds is renowned among Baptist musicians, music ministers, song leaders, and hymnody students. In eminently readable style, David W. Music's comprehensive biography describes Reynolds's family and educational background, his career as a minister of music, denominational leader, and seminary professor.   978-1-57312-690-8 358 pages/pb **$23.00**

With Us in the Wilderness
Finding God's Story in Our Lives
Laura A. Barclay

What stories compose your spiritual biography? In *With Us in the Wilderness*, Laura Barclay shares her own stories of the intersection of the divine and the everyday, guiding readers toward identifying and embracing God's presence in their own narratives.

978-1-57312-721-9 120 pages/pb **$13.00**

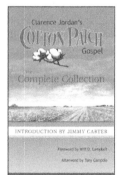

Made in the USA
Coppell, TX
08 November 2021